COOKING DELIGHTS OF THE MAHARAJAS

D1727277

Cooking Delights of
The Maharajas

**EXOTIC DISHES FROM
THE PRINCELY HOUSE OF SAILANA**

Digvijaya Singh

BOOK CREATED BY GOURMET ARTS
8 Shreeniketan
14, M. Karve Marg, Mumbai 400 020

PUBLISHED BY

Vakils, Feffer & Simons Pvt. Ltd.

Hague Building, 9 Sprott Road, Mumbai 400 001

First Edition : 1982
Second Edition : 1984
Third Edition : 1988
Fourth Edition : 1990
Fifth Edition : 1992
Sixth Edition : 1994
Seventh Edition : 1995
Eighth Edition : 1998
Ninth Edition : 2002
Tenth Edition : 2002

Price Rs. 175/-

ISBN 81-87111-14-3

Published by Bimal A. Mehta for Vakils, Feffer and Simons Pvt. Ltd.
Hague Building, 9 Sprott Road, Ballard Estate, Mumbai 400 001.

Printed by Arun K. Mehta at Vakil & Sons Pvt. Ltd.
Industry Manor, Appasaheb Marathe Marg, Prabhadevi, Mumbai 400 025.

Designed by Vakils Art Department

Photographs by D.F. Poonawala
Rajendra Kumar Singh

To the memory of my Father
His Late Highness
Raja Sir Dilip Singhji K.C.I.E.
of Sailana
this book is respectfully dedicated.

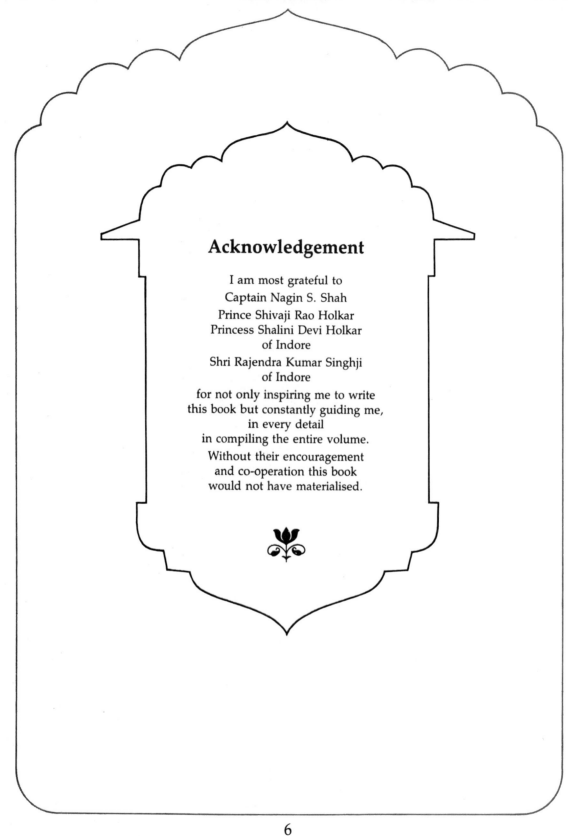

Acknowledgement

I am most grateful to
Captain Nagin S. Shah
Prince Shivaji Rao Holkar
Princess Shalini Devi Holkar
of Indore
Shri Rajendra Kumar Singhji
of Indore

for not only inspiring me to write
this book but constantly guiding me,
in every detail
in compiling the entire volume.

Without their encouragement
and co-operation this book
would not have materialised.

Foreword

It is a pleasure to write this foreword for the Maharaja Saheb of Sailana's book on Indian cuisine particularly as he is most competent to write such a book as he is not only a gourmet but a superb cook.

The author cooks for pleasure and with his vast experience and knowledge of cooking I feel sure that those who buy this book will be introduced to many new and delicious Indian dishes.

Bon Apetit.

Gayatri Devi
Her Highness Rajmata of Jaipur

Contents

Chicken Dishes

Fish Dishes

Game Dishes

Rice and Allied Dishes

Vegetable Dishes

Recipes in Pictures
on the following pages

Preface

Recently, there has been a flood of Indian cook books. While in their own way all are good, I feel, they are aimed at the amateur cook, the busy housewife, who desires to put up a good meal in a hurry. The prices and general pressures of life have done their own damage. Time is scarce and so is leisure. Everyone seeks short-cuts, thereby reducing a precious fine art to the level of plain belly filling. As a result the recipes have become simplified and also to an extent westernised.

In India, with our ancient heritage and many cultures have inherited a variety of cuisine, incomparable and unsurpassable. The Persian School of cooking has had the greatest impact on our cooking. The Maharajas, I know, invariably were connoisseurs of good food. Fine kitchens were maintained and the best cooks sought. Sometimes there was a cook for each recipe. Among them it was a status symbol as to whose table provided the most unusual and luxurious fare. The cooks kept their recipes jealously guarded secrets and the precious formulas often went from father to son. Those not passed on are lost forever.

My father, His Highness Raja Sir Dilip Singhji, K.C.I.E. of Sailana foresaw this eighty years ago and began collecting recipes. It was an all consuming interest which he brought to scientific perfection. He took great pains over each recipe, refining and experimenting again and again till he brought it to perfection. He called cooks from all over to learn from them. He had ancient recipe books in Sanskrit, Urdu and Persian translated. The recipes in this book are the result of his untiring research. I have also maintained and continued this culinary research and am pleased to offer, to those discerning lovers of good food, some of the recipes from our collection.

The *masalas* (spices) are the same as used all over; their quantity and the order in which they are used make all the difference. It is absolutely essential to carefully measure the ingredients and follow the recipes faithfully. Without this, perfection is impossible.

The recipes given here are in their pure form. This book is not for the novice. I have taken for granted that anyone attempting to cook from these has the basic knowledge of cooking. I have however explained certain basic terms and methods which are often misunderstood. It has been quite difficult at times to explain certain Indian terms and methods in English. I have done my best and I keep myself always open for any suggestions.

The dishes given here should delight the palates of the severest critics and gourmets. Before bringing out this book I felt that if such a step is not taken, in a decade or so, the fine art of Indian cooking would vanish beyond revival.

Digvijaya Singh

The Palace
Sailana
M.P.

Helpful Hints

To enable you to follow these recipes correctly I feel certain classifications of terms and methods are necessary. I am giving below some notes on methods and terms most commonly misunderstood:

Pans

Except for boiling, stainless steel and aluminium pans are to be avoided. Heavy-bottomed brass pans are the best for Indian cooking. All the pans should have a properly fitted lid.

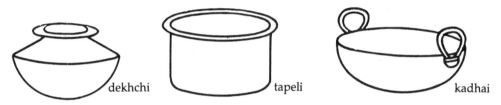

dekhchi   tapeli   kadhai

For meats I prefer *dekhchi*.

For rice and koftas I use *tapeli*.

For frying, *kadhai* or frying pan according to recommendation in recipe.

Pressure cooker — I find this gadget excellent but for boiling only. Use it for dal, rice and to tenderise some very tough meats like trotters and santh.

Weights

The weights given in the recipes are for cleaned, ready to cook vegetables and meats. 1 kg. peas means 1 kg. of shelled peas. Rice, dals etc. are all to be weighed *before* washing or soaking.

Before starting to cook I strongly recommend that the whole recipe should be first read and understood. This would greatly ease the operations. The first step is to look through the recipe to make sure that all the ingredients you need are at hand. Accurate measurements come next. *No guess work — not if you want to be sure of success.* Use standard tea cups and spoons. Measure level; that is, heap up the ingredients, then level off with a knife. Pack down fats.

Bhunao

Bhunao is the process of cooking the ground *masala* at high heat, adding small quantities of liquid (water or *dahi*) just at the moment when the *masala* starts sizzling and sticks to the bottom. The liquid added lowers the cooking temperature and allows you to scrape off the pan's bottom and sides wherever *masala* has started to stick. The process of adding liquid and scraping the barely sticking *masala* is repeated two or three times. It is vital not to let the *masala* burn at the bottom — and this can happen if the cook lets his attention wander for even 15 seconds! The purpose of this *bhunao* process is to have all the *masala* come in contact with the hot pot bottom, giving the ground spices a delicious toasted flavour.

Bhunao is a key to Mughlai cooking, and requires patience and close attention.

Baghar

When aromatic spices such as cloves, cumin seeds or cardamom seeds are dropped into heated oil (or ghee), they release the essence of their flavours into that oil, which is called a *baghar*. The same is true of condiments such as fresh chillies or garlic buds.

The process is the same. The oil is heated almost to smoking in a shallow pan. The heat/flame is reduced to medium and the spices and/or condiments are tossed in. As soon as the ingredients begin to change colour and float upon the oil the pan is removed from the fire. This oil, full of flavour, can be added at the beginning of cooking or at the completion of cooking according to the recipe.

Dhungar

Dhungar (smoked) is a technique of imparting a smoky flavour to a dish. When a particular dish has finished cooking, a live coal is taken and ghee is poured on it, when it starts to smoke this is put in the pot. The smoke from the coal must be trapped in the pot by tightly closing the lid. The smoke, thus trapped for about 30 minutes, permeates the cooked food. Occasionally the *dhungar* flavour is enhanced by first sprinkling spices on the live coal and then adding ghee and covering. The three methods of giving *dhungar* are given below:

Method No. 1: Take a live coal, blow ashes from it, hold it over the pot and pour a little ghee on it. When it starts smoking put the coal in the pot over the cooked dish and cover.

Method No. 2: Take an iron *katori* and place it in the centre of the cooked dish. Put the live coal in it then put the recommended spice on the burning coal. Over the spice put a little ghee and cover. Throw away the coal while serving. The ghee may be added to the preparation.

Method No. 3: This is for dry dishes like *Keema* etc. Instead of metal *katori* as in Method No. 2, take a large onion peel and place the live coal in it. The meat should first be arranged in a circle and the *dhungar* given in the middle.

Dum

This process may be described as the 'maturing of a prepared dish.' After completion of the cooking process, the pot is sealed as tightly as possible, either with dough or with a weighted lid. This pot is then placed on hot ashes and a few coals placed on the lid. It remains thus for thirty minutes, allowing the individual flavours of the dish to blend into their own unique flavour.

A minute amount of water left in the pot before sealing prevents burning and produces steam, which enhances the blending process. The pot should be opened at table so that everyone can benefit from that first and most rarified fragrance.

Kalia and Korma

A vague term in use for these has been 'Curry'. Basically there are two kinds — Kalia and Korma. Kalia is curry with water or milk base, where the gravy contains water. Korma has ghee or oil base, where all water has at the end of cooking been evaporated and only oil or ghee remains.

Do Peeaza

The common error regarding this much used term is that Do Peeaza is where two onions have been used or where the quantity of onions is equal to that of meat. Both are wrong. Do Peeaza, a Moghul term, means any meat cooked with a vegetable like — Do Peeaza Gobi or Do Peeaza Matar.

Pulao

There are two methods of cooking rice. Rice is cooked either in water or in *yakhni* (meat stock). When cooked in meat stock it is known as Pulao.

Yakhni

Yakhni is stock. When meat or vegetables together with spices are boiled and the water is strained through muslin this is known as *yakhni* and is used for cooking Pulao.

Biryani

When rice is first cooked in water, and meat and other things added later in layers and all served together it is known as Biryani.

Water and its use

Water hardness varies from place to place. It is therefore not possible for me to exactly specify the quantity of water in my recipes. One's own judgement will have to be used. Only thing is one should be careful of over-watering! *Adding warm water at any stage does not spoil anything.*

To grind any oily substance like fried onions and garlic or almonds, *khus khus* etc., it is best to grind these with a little sprinkling of water. This not only eases the operation but improves the blending quality and also prevents the oil from separating while grinding.

Garam Masala

"*Garam Masala* Powder" is mentioned in many of my recipes. There are many kinds of powdered *garam masalas* available in the market. Cooks also have their individual recipes. I am giving below my recipe that I have found most satisfactory.

1.	Black cumin seeds	6 gms.	7.	Cinnamon	6 gms.
2.	Cumin seeds	6 gms.	8.	Pepper corns	6 gms.
3.	Cloves	6 gms.	9.	Mace	3 gms.
4.	Bay leaves	6 gms.	10.	Dry ginger	3 gms.
5.	Black cardamom seeds	6 gms.	11.	Saffron (optional)	
6.	Cardamom	6 gms.			

Pound together and sieve through muslin.

Hindi Names for Ingredients

English	Hindi
Almond	Badam
Alum	Phitkari
Amarnth leaves	Chaulai
Ani seeds	Sonf
Asafoetida	Hing
Ash gourd	Petha
Bathwa	Bathwa
Bay leaves	Tej patta
Beetroot	Chukandar
Bitter gourd	Karela
Black cardamom	Badi illaichi
Black cumin seed	Shah jira
Black beans	Urad
Brinjal	Baingan
Buttermilk	Chhas
Cabbage	Bandha gobi
Cardamom	Illaichi
Carrot	Gajar
Carom seeds	Ajwain
Cashewnuts	Kaju
Chironji (small round nuts)	Charoli
Cauliflower	Phool gobi
Cinnamon	Dalchini
Cloves	Loung
Cluster beans	Guwar phali
Coconut	Nariyal
Colocasia	Arvi
Colocasia leaves	Arvi patte
Coriander seeds	Dhania
Coriander leaves	Hara dhania
Cumin seeds	Jeera
Curry leaves	Meetha neem patta
Cuttle bone	Samandar jhag
Dry apricot	Khubani
Dry fig	Anjeer
Dry ginger	Soonth
Dry plums	Alu bukhara (khushk)
Elephant's foot yam	Suran
Fenugreek leaves	Methi
Fenugreek seeds	Methi dana
A flavouring agent used in preparing seekh-kabab etc.	Kachri
Fresh corn	Makka
Fresh green gram	Hara chana
Fresh mint leaves	Hara podina
Garlic	Lahasun
Ginger	Adrak
Gram flour	Besan
Green chillies	Hari mirch
Green coconut	Hara nariyal
Green mango dry	Amchur
Indian cream cheese	Panir
Jack fruit	Kathal
A variety of gooseberry wild growth	Karonda
Lentil red	Masur dal

Lime	**Nimboo**	Powdered mixture	**Garam masala**
Cream top of milk	**Malai**	of cloves,	
		cardamom,	
Mace	**Javitri**	cinnamon and	
Marrow	**Doodhi**	other spices	
Millet	**Bajra**	Ridge gourd	**Turai**
Molasses	**Gur**		
Mustard oil	**Sarson ka tel**	Semolina	**Sujji**
Mustard seeds	**Rai**	Seedless raisins	**Kismis**
		Sesame seeds	**Til**
Nigella	**Kalonji**	Sesame oil	**Til ka tel**
Nutmeg	**Jaiphal**	Sheep's trotters	**Paya**
		Split gram	**Chana dal**
Okra	**Bhindi**	Solidified milk	**Khoa/mawa**
Onion	**Peeaz**	Split green beans	**Moong dal**
Panjabi vadi	**Panjabi vadi**	Tamarind	**Imli**
Parched gram	**Bhuna chana**	Tamarind flower	**Imli ke phool**
Papaya green	**Papita hara**	Turmeric	**Haldi**
Parwal	**Parwal**	Turnip	**Salgam**
Pepper corn	**Kali mirch**		
Peanuts	**Moongphali**	Vermicelli	**Sewain**
Pistachio	**Pista**		
Poppy seeds	**Khus khus**	Walnut	**Akhrot**
		Wild fig	**Goolar**
Radish	**Muli**		
Red chillies	**Lal mirchi**	Yam	**Ratalu**
Red pumpkin	**Kaddu**	Yellow lentils	**Toowar dal**
Refined flour	**Maida**	Yellow mustard	**Sarson**
		seeds	
Powdered rice	**Chawal ka atta**	Paper thin leaf of	**Varak**
		beaten silver	

Weights and Measures

tsp. = teaspoon (level) • tbsp. = tablespoon (level) • pcs. = pieces

Ingredient	3 gms.	6 gms.	9 gms.	12 gms.	25 gms.	60 gms.	120 gms.
Almonds whole				10 pcs.			
Almonds sliced				1½ tbsp.			
Apricots dry				3 pcs.			
Alum		2 tsp.					
Ani seeds	2 tsp.						
Black cardamom	6 pcs.						
Black cumin seeds	2 tsp.						
Cardamom	20 pcs.						
Carom seeds	2 tbsp.						
Cashewnuts				10 pcs.			
Cinnamon	6 pcs. 2″						
Charoli whole		1 tbsp.					
Cloves whole	30 pcs.						
Coconut grated	2 tsp.					½ cup	
Coriander seeds		1 tbsp.					
Coriander seed powder	2 tsp.	4 tsp.	6 tsp.	8 tsp.			
Coriander leaves chopped		1½ tbsp.					
Cumin seeds	1½ tsp.	3 tsp.		6 tsp.			
Curd						⅕ cup	⅖ cup
Cuttle bone (powdered)	1 tsp.						
Figs dry		1 pc.					
Fenugreek seeds	1 tsp.						
Garam masala powder	1½ tsp.	3 tsp.		6 tsp.			
Garlic chopped				1 tbsp.			
Garlic ground		1 tsp.		2 tsp.	4 tsp.		
Ghee				1 tbsp.			½ cup
Ginger chopped				½ tbsp.			
Ginger ground		1 tsp.		2 tsp.	4 tsp.		
Ginger dry powder	1½ tsp.						
Gram flour		1 tbsp.					
Green chillies whole		2 pcs.					
Kachri powdered		1 tbsp.					
Khoa mashed				1 tbsp.			
Mace (Javitri) whole	2 tsp.						
Malai						4 tsp.	⅖ cup

Ingredient	3 gms.	6 gms.	9 gms.	12 gms.	25 gms.	60 gms.	120 gms.
Mangoes green dried	1 tsp.						
Mint leaves		1½ tbsp.					
Molasses (gur)				1 tbsp.	2 tbsp.	⅕ cup	
Mustard whole	1 tsp.						
Mustard yellow whole	1 tsp.						
Nigella whole	2 tsp.						
Nutmeg		2 nuts					
Oil				1 tbsp.		½ cup	
Onions chopped				1 tbsp.			½ cup
Onions ground			1 tsp.		1 tbsp.	3 tbsp.	⅖ cup
Onions sliced							1 cup
Panjabi badi powdered				4 tsp.			
Papad khar powder		2 tsp.					
Papaya raw ground				1 tsp.			
Parched gram powdered				1 tbsp.			
Pepper corns whole	60 pcs.						
Pistachio whole				60 pcs.			
Pistachio sliced				4 tsp.			
Poppy seeds	1½ tsp.	3 tsp.		6 tsp.	3 tbsp.		
Raisins whole				40 pcs.			
Red chillies whole	6 pcs.						
Red chillie powder	2 tsp.	4 tsp.	6 tsp.	8 tsp.			
Refined flour		1 tsp.					
Rice flour				1 tbsp.			
Sajji		2 tsp.					
Salt	¾ tsp.	1½ tsp.	2 tsp.	3 tsp.			
Semolina (suji)				1 tbsp.			
Sesame seeds	1 tsp.			2½ tbsp.			
Sugar	1 tsp.			3 tsp.		⅕ cup	⅖ cup
Tamarind				2 tbsp. pulp			
Turmeric	2 tsp.	4 tsp.	6 tsp.	8 tsp.			

Lime juice 15 mls.=1 tbsp. • Milk 125 mls.=½ cup

1

Tar Kalia

"Tar" means rich. Ideal for festive occasions. To be eaten with chapati or rice.

Preparation time: 30 minutes ● Cooking time: 1½ hours ● To serve: 4 – 6 persons.

½ kg. Mutton pieces
120 gms. Ghee
60 gms. Onions thinly and evenly sliced
15 gms. Salt
12 gms. Red chillies powdered
12 gms. Coriander seeds powdered
3 gms. Cumin seeds powdered

12 gms. Ginger scraped and ground
115 gms. Curd
12 gms. Almonds blanched and ground with water
12 gms. Poppy seeds ground with water
12 gms. Pistachios blanched and ground with water
12 gms. Coconut grated and ground with water

25 gms. Khoa
1½ gms. *Garam masala* powder
A pinch of Saffron diluted in warm water
7 mls. (¼ oz.) Lime juice
15 mls. (½ oz.) Kewada water.

● Heat the ghee and fry sliced onions to a golden brown. Remove, grind dry and keep aside.
● In the same ghee add meat along with salt, red chillies, coriander seeds, cumin seeds, ginger and curd, and *bhunao* thrice. Add ground almonds, poppy seeds, pistachios, coconut and khoa, and once again *bhunao* thrice or till the meat is well-browned. Add fried ground onions.
● Add water, cover and cook till meat is tender. Simmer on low heat till the gravy is thick and ghee floats on top of it.
● Add the *garam masala*, saffron, lime juice and kewada water, and stir.

2

Kalia Saphed (White)*

The unusualness of this ancient Rajasthani recipe lies in the fact that all ingredients used are white.

Preparation time: 30 minutes ● Cooking time: 1½ hours ● To serve: 4 – 6 persons.

½ kg. Mutton pieces
120 gms. Ghee
120 gms. Curd
12 gms. Salt
12 gms. Seeds of red chillies ground with water
12 gms. Ginger scraped and shredded

12 gms. Almonds blanched and ground with water
12 gms. Poppy seeds ground with water
12 gms. Coconut scraped and ground with water
30 gms. Khoa

120 mls. (4 ozs.) Milk
15 mls. (½ oz.) Rose water
7 mls. Lime juice
1½ gms. Cardamom seeds powdered.

● Boil the meat in plenty of water with a little salt for five minutes. Discard water and wash the meat twice in fresh water. Heat the ghee and add meat along with curd, salt, seeds of red chillies and ginger and so much water that it should dry up when meat is tender. Add almonds, poppy seeds, coconut, khoa and milk, and stir. Put on *dum*. When gravy becomes thick and ghee floats on top of it, add rose water, lime juice and cardamom powder.

● For top decoration, pieces of empty shells of red chillies and separately boiled green chilli pieces can be used.

* Picture on page 33.

3

Kalia Razala

This recipe hails from the kitchens of one of the Begums of Bhopal. The aromatic and unique flavour lingers for a long time.

Preparation time: 30 minutes ● Cooking time: $1\frac{1}{2}$ hours ● To serve: 4 – 6 persons.

$\frac{1}{2}$ kg. Mutton pieces from leg	225 gms. Curd	6 gms. Cumin seeds roasted dry and powdered.
225 gms. Ghee	120 gms. Fresh coriander leaves chopped	
225 gms. Green chillies cut lengthwise and seeds removed	60 gms. Ginger scraped and shredded	
225 gms. Onions thinly and evenly sliced	12 gms. Garlic ground	
	18 gms. Salt	

● Melt ghee in the pan and put meat and all the ingredients in it and mix well. No water to be added. Close the pan with tight lid and seal the edges of the pan with wheat flour paste. Also put some weight on the lid to keep it tight.

● Cook on medium fire for one hour. Then open the lid, stir a little and serve.

● This tastes best when cooked in an earthen pot.

4

Kalia Shafak Sheer

'Shafak' means pleasant looking and 'Sheer' means milk. Combines well with rice.

Preparation time: 30 minutes • Cooking time: $1\frac{1}{2}$ hours • To serve: 4 – 6 persons.

$\frac{1}{2}$ kg. Mutton pieces from leg *or* shoulder
120 gms. Ghee
3 gms. Black cardamoms whole
3 gms. Pepper corns whole
60 gms. Onions thinly and evenly sliced

12 gms. Salt
12 gms. Red chillies powdered
12 gms. Ginger scraped and ground
1 litre Milk
20 gms. Almonds blanched and ground with water
12 gms. Rice powdered

12 gms. Coriander seeds powdered
60 gms. Ghee for *baghar*
3 gms. Cloves whole
$1\frac{1}{2}$ gms. *Garam masala* powder
1 tbsp. Fresh coriander leaves chopped.

• Heat the ghee and add cardamoms and pepper corns. Then add sliced onions and fry till golden brown. Add meat, red chillies, salt and ginger. *Bhunao* twice. Then add only as much water that it should dry up when meat is tender. Extra water can be added later on, if required, to make the meat tender.

• Then add milk, ground almonds, rice powder, coriander powder, and stir well. Cover and cook on medium fire till the gravy becomes thick and ghee films the surface. Add *garam masala* powder.

• In a separate pan heat the ghee for *baghar*. Add cloves and when they turn dark brown, add the ghee with cloves to the meat and stir. Add coriander leaves.

Kalia Amba (Mangoes)

A rare Moghul sweet and sour recipe attributed to Emperor Jahangir. Being seasonal, it is said to ward off heat strokes.

Preparation time: 30 minutes ● Cooking time: 1½ hours ● To serve: 4 – 6 persons.

½ kg. Lean mutton from saddle *or* leg, cut into pasandas
120 gms. Ghee
120 gms. Onions thinly and evenly sliced
18 gms. Salt

25 gms. Coriander seeds powdered
25 gms. Ginger scraped and ground
3 gms. *Garam masala* powder

½ kg. Raw mangoes peeled and cut into 1″ thick long slices
250 gms. Sugar
3 gms. Mace ground.

● Prepare meat pasandas as described in Recipe No. 8, cut into 2″ pieces.
● Heat the ghee and fry sliced onions to a golden brown. Add meat along with salt, ground coriander seeds and ginger. *Bhunao* thrice. Add only as much water that it should dry up when meat is tender. Extra water can be added later on, if required, to make the meat tender. When tender, add *garam masala* powder.
● Fork the mango slices. Boil them in water till half-cooked. Drain and discard water.
● In a separate pan put sugar and dilute it with 2 tablespoons of water. Cook on low fire and prepare syrup of two-string consistency. Add mango pieces and mace, and stir. Cook on low fire till the syrup dries up. Put mango pieces on top of the meat. Add one cup of hot water. Put on *dum* till ghee films on the surface of the gravy.

Kalia Badam

Very invigorating and given in the old days after sickness for recuperation. May prove little hard on present stomachs!

Preparation time: 30 minutes • Cooking time: 1½ hours • To serve: 4 – 6 persons.

½ kg. Mutton pieces from leg *or* shoulder
120 gms. Curd
120 gms. Ghee
60 gms. Green coconut for extracting milk
2 Black cardamoms whole

2 2" Cinnamon sticks whole
4 Cloves whole
120 gms. Onions finely chopped
12 gms. Salt
12 gms. Red chillies powdered

1½ gms. Cumin seeds whole
12 gms. Ginger scraped and ground
60 gms. Almonds blanched and finely ground with water.

- Mix curd into the meat and marinade for an hour.
- Heat the ghee, add cardamoms, cinnamon and cloves and then chopped onions, and fry to a light golden colour.
- Add meat and salt, red chillies, cumin seeds and ginger. Add only as much water that it should dry up when meat is tender. Extra water may be added later on, if required, to make the meat tender.
- Add coconut milk and stir. When it starts boiling, add ground almonds. Reduce the heat to the minimum and simmer till gravy becomes thick and ghee floats on top of it.

Note: For extracting coconut milk, first grate it, then grind it finely adding one cup of hot water a little at a time. Squeeze through a muslin. Repeat the process to take out milk to the maximum.

7

Kalia Dal

This recipe combines meat and dal and was developed in my own kitchen; goes extremely well with Poories.

Preparation time: 30 minutes ● Cooking time: 1½ hours ● To serve: 4 – 6 persons.

½ kg. Mutton pieces	6 gms. Turmeric	3 gms. *Garam masala* powder
100 gms. Ghee	36 gms. Onions ground	30 mls. (1 oz.) Lime juice
30 gms. Onions thinly and evenly sliced for mutton	18 gms. Garlic ground	75 gms. Ghee for *baghar*
18 gms. Salt	250 gms. Yellow lentils (*Toovar dal*)	30 gms. Onions thinly and evenly sliced for *baghar*.
18 gms. Red chillies powdered	12 gms. Ginger scraped and thinly sliced	
18 gms. Coriander seeds powdered	6 gms. Fresh mint leaves chopped	

● Heat the ghee and fry sliced onions to a golden brown. Add salt, red chillies, coriander seeds, turmeric, onions and garlic, and *bhunao* thrice. Add meat and *bhunao* till well-browned. Add only as much water that it should dry up when meat is half-cooked.

● Add dal and *bhunao* twice. Add water and cook till meat and dal are tender. Add ginger, mint leaves, *garam masala* powder and lime juice, and stir.

● In a separate pan heat the ghee for *baghar* and fry sliced onions to a golden brown. Add ghee along with fried onions to the meat and stir.

● Put on *dum* till gravy is thick and ghee films on the surface.

● *Moong dal* (skinless) can be cooked in the same way.

Pasanda

As the name suggests everyone likes it, specially vegetarians just starting to eat meat—no bones to bother about!

Preparation time: 30 minutes ● Cooking time: 1½ hours ● To serve: 4 – 6 persons.

½ kg. Lean mutton from saddle *or* leg cut into pasandas
120 gms. Curd
15 gms. Salt
12 gms. Red chillies powdered
12 gms. Coriander seeds powdered
3 gms. Turmeric

3 gms. Cumin seeds whole
3 gms. Fenugreek (*Methi*) leaves dried *or* 12 gms. Fresh leaves finely chopped
6 gms. Green chillies finely chopped and seeds removed
60 gms. Onions ground
25 gms. Garlic ground

12 gms. Ginger scraped and ground
115 gms. Ghee
4 Black cardamoms whole
8 Cloves whole
2 2″ Cinnamon sticks whole
115 gms. Onions thinly and evenly sliced.

● Remove all the white membranes from the surface of the meat. Cut ½″ thick strips and about 2″ square. Beat each piece with the back of a knife or wooden hammer, wetting knife or hammer with a little water to avoid sticking, till they are flattened out and fibres are broken. Meat thus cut and beaten is called 'Pasanda'.

● Mix curd, salt, chillies, coriander seeds, turmeric, cumin seeds, fenugreek leaves, green chillies, ground onions, garlic and ginger into the meat and marinade for half an hour.

● Heat the ghee and add cardamoms, cloves and cinnamon. Add sliced onions and fry to a golden brown. Remove the pan from the fire. Add meat spreading the pieces flat and evenly. Add one cup water. Cover and cook on medium heat. When tender and very little water remains, put on *dum* till water dries up and only ghee remains.

Pasanda Shahi

I am grateful to His Highness Maharaja Ajit Singhji of Jhabua for giving me this fine recipe.

Preparation time: 30 minutes ● Cooking time: 1 hour ● To serve: 4 – 6 persons.

½ kg. Lean mutton from saddle and leg cut into pasandas
115 gms. Ghee
115 gms. Curd
 12 gms. Salt
  9 gms. Red chillies powdered
  6 gms. Coriander seeds powdered
  3 gms. *Garam masala* powder

3 gms. Cumin seeds powdered
6 2" Cinnamon sticks whole
4 Black cardamoms whole
10 Cloves whole
1½ gms. Cardamom seeds powdered
6 gms. Ginger scraped and shredded
6 gms. Ginger scraped and ground

9 gms. Dry figs (*Sukha anjeer*) ground with water
9 gms. Raisins (*Kismish*) ground with water
15 gms. Khoa
15 mls. (½ oz.) Vinegar.
A pinch of Saffron diluted in warm water
A pinch of Asafoetida diluted in water.

● Prepare meat pasandas as described in Recipe No. 8.
● Mix all the ingredients, except ghee, into the meat and marinade for an hour.
● Heat the ghee and add meat, spreading the pieces flat and evenly. No water to be added.
● Close the pan with tight lid and seal the edges of the lid with wheat flour paste. On low heat cook for an hour. Open the lid and, if still some liquid remains, put on *dum* till liquid dries up and only ghee remains.

Korma Shahjehani

One taste of this excellent recipe tells us what a connoisseur of food Shahjehan must have been!

Preparation time: 30 minutes • Cooking time: 1½ hours • To serve: 4 – 6 persons.

½ kg. Mutton pieces from leg *or* shoulder
12 gms. Salt
3 gms. Red chillies powdered
3 gms. Kachri ground with water
6 gms. Ginger scraped and ground
6 gms. Almonds blanched and ground with water

6 gms. Pistachios blanched and ground with water
6 gms. Poppy seeds ground with water
12 gms. Dry figs ground with water
6 gms. Coconut grated and ground with water
6 gms. Parched grams powdered
6 gms. *Garam masala* powdered

3 gms. Nutmeg powdered
4 gms. Cardamoms powdered
A good pinch of Saffron diluted in warm water
120 gms. Curd
120 gms. Ghee
60 gms. Onions thinly and evenly sliced.

• Mix thoroughly all the ingredients, except ghee and onions, into the meat and marinade for two hours.

• Heat the ghee and fry sliced onions to a golden brown. Add the marinaded meat and stir. No water to be added. Close the pan with tight lid and seal the edges of the lid with wheat flour paste. On a very low heat cook for hour and a half.

• Open the lid and, if meat is tender and still some liquid remains, put on hot ashes and place live charcoals on top of the lid, and simmer till liquid dries up and only ghee remains, same as putting on *dum*.

11

Kalia Kesar*

Another favourite of Moghul kings on their excursions to Kashmir. A delicacy for winter time.

Preparation time: 30 minutes ● Cooking time: 1½ hours ● To serve: 4 – 6 persons.

½ kg. Mutton pieces	30 gms. Almonds blanched and ground with water	1½ gms. Saffron diluted in warm water
120 gms. Ghee	115 gms. Curd	1½ gms. Yellow colour powder (edible)
30 gms. Onions thinly and evenly sliced	9 gms. Salt	
30 gms. Coriander seeds powdered	60 gms. *Malai*	15 mls. (½ oz.) Kewada water.
30 gms. Garlic ground	A good pinch of *garam masala* powder	

● Heat the ghee and fry sliced onions to a golden brown. Remove, grind with water and keep aside.

● In the same ghee add meat along with coriander seeds, garlic and almonds, and *bhunao* with curd, adding a little at a time till it finishes. Add water and cook. When meat is tender and about one cup of liquid remains, remove from fire.

● Remove the meat from the liquid. In a separate cup of water dip the meat pieces to remove whatever *masala* is left over the pieces. Keep the meat aside. The above water should be added to the liquid in which meat was cooked. Strain the liquid through muslin, squeezing well to extract maximum flavour.

● Put the meat and the strained liquid back into the pan. Add fried ground onions and salt.

● In a separate pan mix thoroughly *malai,* saffron, yellow colour and kewada water and then add to the meat, and stir.

● Put on *dum* till ghee films on the surface of the gravy.

Top: Korma Khada Masale ka
Mid-left: Kalia Saphed
Mid-right: Kalia Kesar
Bottom: Korma Asafjahi

* *Picture on facing page.*

12

Korma Shirazi*

A fine example of the Persian School of Cooking. Shiraz in Persia must have been what Paris is to the Western World. A fountainhead of fine foods.

Preparation time: 30 minutes • Cooking time: 1½ hours • To serve: 4 persons.

½ kg. Mutton pieces from leg *or* shoulder
175 gms. Ghee
60 gms. Onions thinly and evenly sliced
15 gms. Salt
12 gms. Coriander seeds powdered
12 gms. Red chillies powdered
3 gms. Turmeric

3 gms. Pepper corns powdered
18 gms. Ginger scraped and ground
1½ gms. Cardamom seeds powdered
12 gms. Almonds whole blanched
12 gms. Pistachios whole blanched

12 gms. Apricots (*Khubani*) dry, whole, soaked in water and stones removed
12 gms. Raisins whole
A pinch of Saffron diluted in water
4 Eggs hard-boiled and cut into halves.

• Heat the ghee, add sliced onions and fry them to a golden brown. Add meat along with salt, red chillies, coriander seeds, turmeric, pepper corns and ginger. *Bhunao* 4–5 times or till the meat is well-browned.

• Add water, cover and cook. When meat is tender and very little water remains, add cardamom, almonds, pistachios, apricots, raisins and saffron. Reduce the heat to the minimum and put some live charcoals on top of the lid. Simmer till water dries up and only ghee remains.

• While serving add sliced eggs.

Top: Do Peeaza Borani
Mid-left: Be Masale ka Korma
Mid-right: Korma Shirazi
Bottom: Seekh Kabab Korma

* Picture on facing page.

Korma Ahmedshahi

I am grateful to His Excellency Colonel Suberna Sham Sher Jung Bahadur Rana for giving me this fine recipe. Ahmedshah was employed as drama coach in his Court at Nepal and was, I am told, a better cook than dramatist.

Preparation time: 30 minutes • Cooking time: 1½ hours • To serve: 4 – 6 persons.

½ kg. Mutton pieces from leg and shoulder
125 gms. Ghee
120 gms. Onions finely and evenly sliced
9 gms. Salt
120 gms. Curd

12 gms. Ginger scraped and ground
12 gms. Coriander seeds powdered
3 gms. Cumin seeds powdered
1½ gms. Ani seeds (*Sonf*) powdered
2 Black cardamoms powdered

20 Pepper corns powdered
5 2" Cinnamon sticks powdered
10 Cloves powdered
One pinch of Saffron diluted in warm water
15 mls. (½ oz.) Kewada water.

• Heat the ghee and fry sliced onions to a golden brown. Add meat and salt. Cover and cook till the meat juices dry up, then add only as much water that it should dry up when meat is tender.

• Beat the curd and mix in it all the remaining ingredients. Add into meat and stir well. Put on *dum* till curd dries up and only ghee remains.

Korma Asafjahi*

Hyderabad has always been known for its excellent cuisine. This recipe was given to my grandfather by the Nizam in 1905.

Preparation time: 30 minutes ● Cooking time: 1½ hours ● To serve: 4 – 6 persons.

½ kg. Mutton pieces from leg *or* shoulder
115 gms. Ghee
12 gms. Salt
12 gms. Garlic ground
12 gms. Ginger scraped and ground
25 gms. Almonds blanched and sliced
12 gms. Raisins (*Kismish*) whole

60 gms. Onions finely chopped
6 gms. Red chillies powdered
1½ gms. Pepper corns powdered
1½ gms. *Garam masala* powder
6 gms. Sugar

25 gms. Green chillies finely chopped without seeds
A pinch of Saffron diluted in warm water
1 tbsp. Fresh coriander leaves chopped
250 gms. Curd fresh and thick.

● Put the curd in a muslin and hang it on a peg for two hours. Then whip it and keep aside.
● Heat half of the ghee, add garlic and ginger and fry till golden brown. Add meat and salt, and *bhunao* thrice. Add only as much water that it should dry up when meat is tender. Keep aside.
● In a separate pan heat remaining half of the ghee. Fry almonds and raisins separately to a golden colour and keep aside. In the same ghee fry chopped onions to a golden brown, add red chillies, pepper corns, *garam masala* powder, sugar and green chillies, and cook with 2 tablespoonsfuls of water, stirring well till water dries up. Add to the meat and stir. Add almonds, raisins, curd, saffron and coriander leaves, and stir well. Simmer on low heat for five minutes only and serve immediately.

* *Picture on page 33.*

Korma Khada Masale ka*

This Korma when cooked is most colourful. All the Masalas appear khada or whole. This recipe in the present form was developed by my father and used for all State Banquets. It is not only decorative but I can say one of the finest dishes to come from Sailana. It is served in plates and the display of meat, eggs, onions, etc. is most colourful.

Preparation time: 30 minutes • Cooking time: 1½ hours • To serve: 4 – 6 persons.

½ kg. Mutton leg muscles
170 gms. Ghee
4 Black cardamoms whole
10 Cloves whole
2 Bay leaves whole
60 gms. Onions thinly and evenly sliced
115 gms. Curd
15 gms. Salt
6 gms. Red chillies powdered
6 gms. Red chillies whole
12 gms. Coriander seeds powdered

3 gms. Cumin seeds whole
18 gms. Ginger scraped and shredded
100 gms. Onions small, whole, peeled
50 gms. Garlic whole, peeled
12 gms. Green chillies cut into two pieces
One good pinch of saffron diluted in warm water

30 mls. (1 oz.) Fresh lime juice
1 tbsp. Fresh coriander leaves chopped
4 Eggs hard-boiled, shelled and cut into halves
225 gms. Green peas fresh and shelled
6 gms. Salt for green peas.

• Heat the ghee, add cardamoms, cloves and bay leaves. Then add sliced onions and fry them to a golden brown. Add meat along with curd, salt, red chillies powder, red chillies whole, coriander seeds, cumin seeds and ginger and enough water to cook the meat. When meat is tender and very little water remains, add whole onions, garlic and green chillies, and cook on low heat. While stirring be careful not to break the onions and garlic. When onions are tender and water dries up, add separately cooked peas, saffron, lime juice and coriander leaves, and stir gently. While serving add pieces of eggs.

• Boil peas separately with salt and add only as much water that it should dry up when peas are tender but not mushy.

* Picture on page 33.

16

Korma Loabdar

Use of Gum and its energizing effects in Indian cooking and medicines are well known. This recipe provides all the goodness plus excellent meaty flavour.

Preparation time: 30 minutes ● Cooking time: 1½ hours ● To serve: 4 persons.

½ kg. Mutton leg muscles
115 gms. Ghee
4 Black cardamoms whole

2 2" Cinnamon sticks whole
6 Cloves whole

2 Bay leaves whole
9 gms. Salt
6 gms. Gum crystals white.

● Heat the ghee. Add cardamoms, cinnamon, cloves and bay leaves. Stir for a minute. Remove and discard.
● In the same ghee add meat, and *bhunao* thrice. Add salt and enough water to cook the meat. When meat is tender and very little water remains, add gum, well diluted in warm water and stir.
● Put on *dum* till the liquid dries up completely and only ghee remains.

17

Be Masale ka Korma*

This is an unusual Korma, made without spices. It has its own unique flavour. Easily digestible.

Preparation time: 30 minutes ● Cooking time: 1½ hours ● To serve: 4 persons.

½ kg. Mutton leg muscles
115 gms. Ghee pure

250 gms. Curd well-beaten
9 gms. Salt

7 mls. (¼ oz.) Kewada water.

● Heat the ghee. Add a few drops of water and cover. Repeat this process thrice. This will remove all moisture as well as impurities from the ghee. Remove from fire and cool a bit.
● Add meat along with curd and salt, and cook, covered, on low fire, till the liquids dry up completely. If meat is not tender add water, as necessary, and cook till it is tender.
● *Bhunao* the meat to a light golden colour. Add kewada water.
● This meat preparation can be kept and eaten for several days.

* Picture on page 34.

Korma Achari

One of my children would eat nothing but Achar-Roti. It became a problem to feed any nourishment. It was then I invented this and solved the problem.

Preparation time: 30 minutes ● Cooking time: $1\frac{1}{2}$ hours ● To serve: 4 – 6 persons.

$\frac{1}{2}$ kg. Mutton pieces from leg *or* shoulder
15 gms. Salt
3 gms. Turmeric
25 gms. Mustard oil
100 gms. Ghee
60 gms. Onions finely and evenly sliced
9 gms. Red chillies whole
6 Cloves whole

3 Black cardamoms whole
$1\frac{1}{2}$ gms. Mustard whole
A pinch of Asafoetida (*Hing*) diluted in water
9 gms. Red chillies powdered
3 gms. Cumin seeds whole
$1\frac{1}{2}$ gms. Nigella (*Kalonji*) whole

6 gms. Molasses (*Gur*) diluted in water
12 gms. Ginger scraped and shredded
36 gms. Garlic whole
30 mls. Fresh lime juice.

● Boil the meat with salt and turmeric in only as much water that it should almost dry up when meat is tender. If some liquid remains, drain and use it in *bhunao*.

● In a separate pan heat mustard oil, when it smokes, add ghee. Fry sliced onions to a golden brown, remove and keep aside. In the same oil add red chillies whole, and fry till they turn black, take out and discard. Add cloves and cardamoms. After a while add the mustard, and when it splutters, add asafoetida. Add meat along with red chilli powder, cumin seeds, nigella, molasses, ginger and garlic. *Bhunao* 3–4 times, using meat liquid, if left, or water. Add lime juice and 2 tablespoons of water and simmer on low heat till the liquids dry up and only ghee remains. While serving garnish the meat with the fried onions.

Korma Narendra Shahi

This excellent Korma, with a slight sweet edge in taste, provides a variation admired by many. Specially those who prefer their food less spicy.

Preparation time: 30 minutes ● Cooking time: 1½ hours ● To serve: 4 – 6 persons.

½ kg. Mutton pieces from leg *or* shoulder
150 gms. Ghee
½ kg. Onions thinly and evenly sliced
115 gms. Curd
20 gms. Salt

12 gms. Red chillies powdered
3 gms. Cumin seeds whole
30 gms. Green chillies ground with seeds
A pinch of Saffron diluted in warm water

30 mls. (1 oz.) Rose water
1 tbsp. Fresh coriander leaves chopped
3 gms. *Garam masala* powder.

● Heat the ghee and fry half of the sliced onions to a golden brown. Add meat along with curd, salt, red chillies and cumin seeds and also the remaining sliced onions, and stir well. No water to be added. Cover and cook on medium heat stirring occasionally.

● When meat is tender, add green chillies. Reduce heat to the minimum and put some live charcoals on top of the lid. Simmer till liquids dry up completely and only ghee remains. Add the remaining ingredients and stir.

Seekh Kabab Korma

Another slightly sweet but extremely decorative dish. Can be truly called "Mouth Watering".

Preparation time: 30 minutes • Cooking time: 1½ hours • To serve: 4 – 6 persons.

½ kg. Lean mutton from saddle and leg	150 gms. Ghee	1½ gms. Cardamom seeds powdered
15 gms. Salt	60 gms. Onions thinly and evenly sliced	A pinch of Saffron diluted in warm water
12 gms. Red chillies powdered	2 2" Cinnamon sticks whole	12 to 14 wooden skewers 4" long (bamboo cut into match-stick thickness).
25 gms. Ginger scraped and ground	6 Cloves whole	
	115 gms. Curd	
	40 gms. Raisins cut into halves	

• Remove all the white membranes from the surface of the meat. Cut the meat into 1" thick strips, then cut into 1" square pieces. Beat them with the back of a knife or wooden hammer till they are flattened out.

• Mix salt, red chillies and ginger into the meat and marinade for half an hour. Put 5–6 pieces into each skewer leaving the ends of the skewer clear.

• Heat the ghee and fry sliced onions to a golden brown. Remove from ghee, grind dry and keep aside.

• In the same ghee put cinnamon and cloves. Add meat and *bhunao* 3–4 times taking care not to break the sticks. Add only as much water that it should dry up when meat is tender. Add whipped curd, fried onions, cardamom seeds, raisins and saffron. Simmer on low heat till water dries up and only ghee remains.

• To be served in shallow dishes for proper display.

Do Peeaza Narangi

The tangy orange flavour of this Korma makes it a delight to eat in summer.

Preparation time: 30 minutes ● Cooking time: 1½ hours ● To serve: 4 – 6 persons.

½ kg. Mutton leg muscles
120 gms. Ghee
120 gms. Curd
15 gms. Salt
12 gms. Red chillies powdered

3 gms. Cumin seeds
3 gms. Turmeric
12 gms. Ginger scraped and ground

6 gms. Coriander seeds powdered
360 mls. (12 ozs.) Fresh orange juice.

● Heat the ghee and add meat along with curd, salt, red chillies, cumin seeds, turmeric, ginger and coriander seeds. Cook while stirring occasionally till liquids dry up completely. *Bhunao* 4–5 times or till the meat is well-browned. Add only as much water that it should dry up when meat is half-cooked.

● Oranges should be semi-ripe. Take out juice through a strainer, and add to the meat. Cover and cook on medium heat till meat is tender and very little liquid remains. If necessary, extra water may be added to make the meat tender. Then reduce the heat to the minimum and put some live charcoals on top of the lid. Simmer till the liquid dries up completely and only ghee remains.

Do Peeaza Chukander

Preparation time: 30 minutes ● Cooking time: 1½ hours ● To serve: 4 – 6 persons.

½ kg. Mutton leg muscles
½ kg. Beetroots peeled
120 gms. Ghee
60 gms. Onions thinly and evenly sliced
115 gms. Curd

15 gms. Salt
9 gms. Red chillies powdered
6 gms. Coriander seeds powdered

15 gms. Ginger scraped and ground
3 gms. *Garam masala* powder.

● Cut the beetroots into small pieces. Boil them in so much water that it should almost dry up when cooked. Grind the beetroots to a fine paste. Strain the liquid through a muslin squeezing well to extract maximum flavour. Keep aside.

● Heat the ghee and fry sliced onions to a golden brown. Remove and grind dry. In the same ghee add meat along with curd, salt, red chillies, coriander seeds and ginger, and *bhunao* 2–3 times. Add fried ground onions and enough water to cook the meat. When meat is three-fourths cooked and a little water remains, add beetroot juice; if necessary extra water may be added to make the meat tender. When tender, add *garam masala* powder and simmer on low heat till water dries up and only ghee remains.

23

Do Peeaza Gobhi

Preparation time: 30 minutes • Cooking time: 1½ hours • To serve: 4 – 6 persons.

½ kg. Mutton pieces from leg *or* shoulder	12 gms. Red chillies powdered	12 gms. Green chillies ground with seeds
225 gms. Cauliflower cut into big pieces	25 gms. Ginger scraped and ground	4 Black cardamoms whole
175 gms. Ghee	12 gms. Panjabi badi powdered	6 Cloves whole
115 gms. Curd		2 2″ Cinnamon sticks whole.
15 gms. Salt		

- In ghee fry cauliflower to a golden brown; remove and keep aside.
- In the same ghee add cardamoms, cloves and cinnamon. Add meat along with curd, salt, red chillies and ginger, and *bhunao* 3–4 times. Add water and cook. When meat is tender and very little water remains, add cauliflower, green chillies and Panjabi badi, and stir. Simmer on low heat till water dries up and only ghee remains. After adding cauliflower stir carefully to avoid breaking them.

24

Do Peeaza Lal Mirch

A Rajasthani favourite: I would recommend this recipe only for those who are fond of very hot food.

Preparation time: 30 minutes • Cooking time: 1½ hours • To serve: 4 – 6 persons.

½ kg. Mutton pieces from leg *or* shoulder	60 gms. Onions thinly and evenly sliced	1½ gms. Cumin seeds whole
150 gms. Ghee	115 gms. Curd	6 gms. Coriander seeds powdered
4 Black cardamoms whole	15 gms. Salt	
25 gms. Garlic finely chopped	60 gms. Red chillies whole	225 gms. Onions cut into 1″ pieces.
	1½ gms. Turmeric	

- Cut red chillies whole into two pieces and discard the seeds. Wash.
- Heat the ghee, add cardamoms and chopped garlic, and fry to a golden brown. Add sliced onions and also fry them to a golden brown. Add meat along with all the remaining ingredients. Add only as much water that it dries up when meat is tender. When a little water remains, reduce the heat and simmer till water dries up and only ghee remains.

Do Peeaza Borani*

Preparation time: 30 minutes • Cooking time: 1½ hours • To serve: 4 – 6 persons.

½ kg. Finely minced lean mutton from leg or shoulder
12 gms. Ghee for mutton
9 gms. Salt
12 gms. Coriander seeds powdered
12 gms. Ginger scraped and ground
3 gms. *Garam masala* powder

1 Egg
250 gms. Carrots scraped and halved
115 gms. Ghee for frying carrots
60 gms. Ghee for gravy
115 gms. Onions thinly and evenly sliced
250 gms. Curd fresh and thick

9 gms. Garlic ground
18 gms. Rice powdered
6 gms. Salt
A pinch of Saffron diluted in warm water
60 gms. Ghee for *baghar*
10 Cloves for *baghar*.

• Boil meat in about 4 cups of water with ghee and salt. When meat is tender, dry the liquids completely. Add coriander seeds, ginger and *garam masala* powder. Finely grind the meat. Mix the egg.

• Scrape the carrots, cut and remove both ends, which are hard, uneven or thin. Cut the carrots into halves lengthwise and remove the hard core from the middle.

• Boil in water till tender. Remove and dry them on a cloth. Cool for a while. Coat ground meat evenly over the carrots, wetting hands with a little water to give even and smooth shape. Fry in ghee till well-browned, remove and keep aside.

• In ghee, for the gravy, fry the sliced onions to a golden brown. Remove and grind dry and put back in the ghee, stir and keep warm. Beat the curd well and add in it garlic, rice powder, salt and saffron. Stir well. Pour this mixture into the above ghee and stir. Then add fried carrots in it and stir gently. In a separate pan heat the ghee for *baghar*. Add cloves. When they turn dark brown, put the ghee with cloves into the main dish and stir gently.

• To be served at once. This preparation is not to be reheated.

* *Picture on page 34.*

Tabak Mans

A famous Kashmiri dish of which many versions are available. I tasted many and finally readjusted the proportions to this version.

Preparation time: 30 minutes • Cooking time: 1½ hours • To serve: 4 – 6 persons.

½ kg. Mutton pieces from leg *or* shoulder
115 gms. Curd
12 gms. Red chillies powdered
12 gms. Coriander seeds powdered
3 gms. Cumin seeds powdered
50 gms. Onions ground

12 gms. Garlic ground
12 gms. Ginger scraped and ground
6 Cloves whole
3 Black cardamoms whole
1 2" Cinnamon stick whole
2 Bay leaves whole
120 gms. Ghee
120 gms. Onions thinly and evenly sliced

12 gms. Salt
12 gms. Green chillies ground without seeds
A pinch of Saffron diluted in warm water
1 tbsp. Fresh coriander leaves chopped.

• Boil the meat in water along with curd, red chillies, coriander seeds, cumin seeds, onions, garlic, ginger, cloves, cardamoms, cinnamon, and bay leaves. When half-cooked, remove the meat from the liquid. In a separate bowl of water dip the meat pieces to remove whatever *masala* is left over the pieces. Keep meat aside.

• The above water should be added to the liquid in which meat was boiled. Strain the liquid through a muslin, squeezing well to extract maximum flavour.

• Heat the ghee and fry sliced onions to a golden brown. Remove and grind dry.

• In the same ghee put meat, the strained liquid, salt, and fried ground onions. Cover and cook till meat is tender and very little water remains. Add green chillies, saffron and coriander leaves. Simmer on low heat till water dries up and only ghee remains.

Mans ka Soola

This superb Barbacue hails from Rajasthan. Easy to cook at home or on the battlefield. Goes extremely well in drink parties.

Preparation time: 1½ hours ● Cooking time: 30 minutes ● To serve: 4 – 6 persons.

½ kg. Lean mutton from saddle and leg	60 gms. Onions, thinly and evenly sliced	12 gms. Garlic ground
60 gms. Ghee (preferably pure)	6 gms. Salt	12 gms. Kachri ground with water
	6 gms. Red chillies powdered	3 gms. Raw papaya peeled and ground.

● Clean, wash and wipe the meat. Remove completely all the white membranes from the surface of the meat. With a sharp knife cut ¼″ thin piece and about 2½″×2½″ squares. Gently flatten the pieces by beating both the sides with a wooden hammer or with the back of a heavy knife, wetting hammer or knife with a little water to avoid sticking.

● Heat the ghee and fry sliced onions to a golden brown. Remove and grind with water.

● Mix salt, red chillies, garlic, kachri and raw papaya into the meat. Add fried ground onions and about 30 mls. (1 oz.) cold water. Finally add ghee and mix well.

● Give *dhungar*, method No. 3, of cloves thrice. Marinade the meat for an hour.

● Take a skewer (*seekh*) about 18″ long. Pass the skewer through the centre of each piece of the meat. Pack the pieces closely, levelling the *masala* in between the pieces. With a string tie the pieces, first from one end of the skewer to the other end and then around the pieces, to keep them firm while cooking.

● Light a layer of charcoal and let them burn until white ash appears on the surface. Rest the skewer on some platform, at both ends of fire, so that the meat pieces remain 6 inches above the fire. Keep on rotating the skewer to cook evenly. When meat becomes light brown, reduce heat and keep on rotating till it is tender and well-browned.

● Remove the strings gently, take out the meat pieces, a few at a time, into the serving dish.

● Serve at once.

● Can be made of any game meat. Can be served as a snack also.

Mans ki Kadhi

Preparation time: 30 minutes • Cooking time: 1½ hours • To serve: 6 – 8 persons.

½ kg. Mutton pieces from leg *or* shoulder
12 gms. Salt for mutton
30 gms. Ghee
12 gms. Garlic chopped
3 gms. Cumin seeds
   A pinch of Asafoetida diluted in water
60 gms. Gram flour (*Besan*)

1200 mls. (4 cups) sour buttermilk or sour curd diluted in water
7 gms. Salt
3 gms. Red chillies powdered
1½ gms. Turmeric powdered
60 gms. Onions ground

12 gms. Garlic ground
12 gms. Green chillies chopped with seeds
1½ gms. Cumin seeds powdered
1 tbsp. Fresh coriander leaves chopped.

• Heat the ghee and fry chopped garlic to a golden brown. Add cumin seeds, then meat with salt and asafoetida. Cover and cook till the meat juices dry up. *Bhunao* thrice. Add enough water and cook the meat till it is three-fourths tender.

• In a separate pan mix gram flour in buttermilk and stir till all lumps disappear. Add salt, red chillies, turmeric, onions, garlic and green chillies and about 4 cups of water. Add this mixture to the meat and cook on medium heat. Keep on stirring till it starts boiling, then cover and cook on low heat. Larger utensils (*tapela*) and low heat are recommended to avoid frothing over. When meat is tender and gravy starts getting thick, add cumin seeds powdered and coriander leaves. Give *dhungar*, method No. 1.

• If buttermilk is not sour enough fresh lime juice may be added afterwards according to taste.

• Chicken may be used instead of mutton.

Jungli Mans*

As the name suggests this is a recipe for the stranded Shikari. It has only five ingredients: meat, ghee or oil, salt, whole red chillies and water. These can be available in the remotest village in India. With this method one can cook meat, game, fowl or even potatoes.

Preparation time: 15 minutes • Cooking time: 1½ hours • To serve: 4 persons.

• Heat the ghee or oil and put the meat. After 10 minutes add salt and red chillies whole. Add little water every now and then being careful to maintain a balance that neither the meat should fry nor boil. Both activities should be sort of simultaneous. When tender, dry up the water and eat.

• I have deliberately avoided giving any weight and measures as these are not available when stranded on shikar.

30

Roghan Josh

Every restaurant in India serves Roghan Josh. Originally this is a Kashmiri recipe. After much research I could collect this authentic recipe which offers a unique flavour.

Preparation time: 30 minutes • Cooking time: 1½ hours • To serve: 4 persons.

½ kg. Mutton leg muscles unwashed	115 gms. Curd	4 Black cardamoms powdered
175 gms. Ghee	12 gms. Salt	10 Cardamoms powdered
A piece of Asafoetida the size of a pepper corn diluted in water	9 gms. Red chillies powdered	20 Cloves powdered
18 gms. Ginger scraped and ground	12 gms. Coriander seeds powdered	5 2" Cinnamon sticks powdered
	A pinch of Saffron diluted in warm water	20 Pepper corns powdered.

• Do not wash the meat, clean it with a piece of cloth removing blood and dirt, if any.

• Heat the ghee, add asafoetida and meat. Cover and cook till meat juices dry up. Add curd and ginger, and stir. *Bhunao* thrice.

• Add salt, red chillies and coriander seeds, and *bhunao* till well-browned. Add just sufficient water that it almost dries up when meat is tender. When meat is tender and very little water remains, add all the remaining ingredients. Put on *dum* till water dries up completely and only ghee remains.

* *Picture on facing page.*

Above: Ingredients for Jungli Mans
Below: Cooked Recipe

Musallam (Whole) Badam-Piste ka Salan*

This superb dish is one of the finest examples of the fabulous rich food enjoyed by the Moghul Emperors. The speciality is the almonds become absolutely tender and yet retain their shape.

Preparation time: 45 minutes ● Cooking time: 2 hours ● To serve: 6 – 8 persons.

115 gms. Almonds blanched whole

115 gms. Pistachios blanched whole

16 gms. Alum powdered

6 gms. Sajji powdered

6 gms. Papad khar powdered

120 mls. (4 ozs.) Milk for boiling almonds

175 gms. Ghee

115 gms. Onions thinly and evenly sliced

½ kg. Minced lean mutton from leg *or* shoulder (*Keema*)

18 gms. Salt

12 gms. Red chillies powdered

18 gms. Coriander seeds powdered

30 gms. Ginger scraped and ground

115 gms. Curd

½ litre Milk

115 gms. *Malai*

18 gms. Green chillies finely chopped with seeds

7 gms. *Garam masala* powder

30 mls. (1 oz.) Lime juice
A pinch of Saffron diluted in warm water.

● Boil 4 cups of water. Add blanched almonds and half each of alum, sajji and papad khar. Stir and cover. After half an hour take out the almonds and discard the water. Again take 4 cups of fresh water and boil. Add the almonds and remaining half portion of alum, sajji and papad khar. Stir, cover and boil for half an hour, or till the almonds are tender. Take out the almonds and discard the water. In milk, add almonds, and boil for 5 minutes and discard the milk. This will help removing all the salt from the almonds. Wash the almonds in water.

● Heat the ghee and fry separately almonds and pistachios on a low fire to a light golden colour. Keep aside.

● In the same ghee fry sliced onions to a golden brown. Add minced meat and brown it lightly. Add salt, red chillies, coriander seeds, ginger, curd and milk, and stir. Add almonds and pistachios. Cover and cook on a medium fire. When meat is tender, add the remaining ingredients, and stir. Put on *dum* till the gravy becomes thick and ghee floats on top of it.

Top: Musallam (Whole) Badam-Piste ka Salan
Mid-left: Kabab ki Kadhi
Mid-right: Paya Khushk
Bottom: Kaleji ka Raita   * *Picture on facing page.*

Kabab ki Kadhi*

Preparation time: 30 minutes • Cooking time: 2 hours • To serve: 6 – 8 persons.

Ingredients for Kadhi

- 30 gms. Gram flour (*Besan*)
- 600 mls. (2 cups) sour buttermilk *or* one cup sour curd diluted in water
- 9 gms. Salt
- 1½ gms. Red chillies powdered
- 1½ gms. Turmeric
- 1½ gms. Cumin seeds whole
- 30 gms. Onions ground
- 6 gms. Garlic ground
- 6 gms. Green chillies whole
- 30 gms. Ghee
- 6 gms. Garlic chopped
- A pinch of Asafoetida diluted in water
- 1 tbsp. Fresh coriander leaves chopped

Ingredients for Kabab

- 250 gms. Lean minced mutton from leg *or* shoulder
- 60 gms. Split grams (*Chana dal*)
- 12 gms. Ghee
- 60 gms. Curd
- 12 gms. Salt
- 3 gms. Red chillies powdered
- 6 gms. Coriander seeds powdered
- 1½ gms. Cumin seeds whole
- 12 gms. Green chillies ground without seeds
- 30 gms. Onions ground
- 6 gms. Garlic ground
- 6 gms. Ginger scraped and ground
- Ghee for frying kababs.

• Mix gram flour in buttermilk and stir well till all lumps disappear. Add salt, red chillies, turmeric, cumin seeds, onions, garlic and green chillies and about 2 cups of water. Heat the ghee and fry chopped garlic to a golden brown. Add asafoetida and then the gram flour. Cook on medium fire stirring all the time till it starts boiling. Cover and cook for half an hour. If necessary add more water during the cooking. When cooked, it should be like thick soup. Give *dhungar*, method No. 1. Add chopped coriander leaves. Keep it warm on hot ashes.

• In a separate pan boil minced meat in about 4 cups of water with all the ingredients. When meat is tender, dry the liquids completely. Grind it finely. Make 25 balls and flatten, wetting hands with a little water to give smooth and even shape. Heat the ghee in a frying pan, and shallow fry the kababs, 6–7 at a time, on a medium heat till dark brown in colour. Put the kababs in a serving dish and pour hot kadhi over them and serve immediately.

* Picture on page 52.

Shabdegh

Shab means night and Degh is a short form of Deghchi. As the name suggests this is to be cooked all night. I have found my own shortcut without sacrificing the flavour. Now there is no need to sit and cook all night, just follow this recipe.

Preparation time: 30 minutes ● Cooking time: 1½ hours ● To serve: 4 – 6 persons.

225 gms. Turnips (*Shalgam*) peeled and rounded

3 gms. Salt for turnips

½ kg. Mutton pieces from leg

175 gms. Ghee

60 gms. Onions thinly and evenly sliced

18 gms. Salt

18 gms. Red chillies powdered

18 gms. Onions ground

115 gms. Curd

6 gms. Ginger scraped and ground

6 gms. Panjabi badi powdered

3 gms. Dried green mango powdered

1½ gms. *Garam masala* powder

9 gms. Coriander powdered

A pinch of Saffron diluted in warm water.

● Peel the turnips giving them round shape. Prick them well with a fork. Rub salt over them and put them in sunlight till water stops dripping from the turnips. Wash them well in cold water.

● Heat the ghee and fry sliced onions to a golden brown. Remove and grind dry. In the same ghee add meat with salt, red chillies and onions, and stir. *Bhunao* till meat is well-browned. Then add only as much water that it should dry up when meat is half-cooked. Add turnips and *bhunao* with curd till the curd is used up. Add water and simmer on low heat for about an hour. When meat is tender, add all the remaining ingredients and also fried onions, and stir. Put on hot ashes and live charcoals on top of the lid till ghee floats on top of the gravy.

● Turnips should be tender and of even size.

Malgoba

Preparation time: 30 minutes ● Cooking time: 1½ hours ● To serve: 4 – 6 persons.

½ kg. Mutton pieces from leg *or* shoulder	20 Pepper corns whole	12 gms. Ginger scraped and ground
115 gms. Ghee	12 gms. Salt	½ kg. Curd fresh and thick
60 gms. Onions thinly and evenly sliced	12 gms. Coriander seeds powdered	6 gms. Refined flour (*Maida*)
4 Black cardamoms	12 gms. Red chillies powdered	1 tbsp. Fresh coriander leaves chopped.
20 Cloves whole	3 gms. Turmeric	

● Heat the ghee, add cardamoms, cloves and pepper corns. Then add sliced onions, and fry them to a golden brown. Add meat along with salt, coriander seeds, turmeric, and *bhunao* thrice. Then add red chillies and ginger, and again *bhunao* twice. Add so much water that it should dry up when meat is tender. Mix flour in the curd. Sieve curd through a muslin. Add curd and coriander leaves to the meat and stir. Put on *dum* till ghee films on the surface of the gravy.

Note: Be extra careful about the curd used. It should be absolutely fresh. As curd constitutes the main flavour, bad or smelly curd can ruin the dish.

Musallam (Whole) Raan

This recipe came to us from a very famous cook from Lucknow. It has all the delicate flavouring associated with food of the Nawabs of Oudh.

Preparation time: 30 minutes • Cooking time: 1½ hours • To serve: 6 – 8 persons.

1 kg. Mutton whole leg	9 gms. Pepper corns powdered	1½ Mace (*Javitri*) powdered
115 gms. Ghee	30 gms. Parched grams powdered	25 gms. Raw papaya ground with water
60 gms. Curd		25 gms. Khoa
60 gms. Onions thinly and evenly sliced	9 gms. Almonds blanched and ground with water	2 drops of Kewada essence (*Itra*) or 30 mls. (1 oz.) of kewada water.
18 gms. Salt	9 gms. Poppy seeds (*Khus-khus*) ground with water	A pinch of Saffron diluted in warm water.
9 gms. Red chillies powdered	25 gms. Ginger scraped and ground	
9 gms. Coriander seeds powdered	1½ gms. Cardamom seeds powdered	
3 gms. *Garam masala* powdered		

• Heat the ghee and fry sliced onions to a golden brown. Remove, grind and keep aside.

• Remove all the white membranes from the surface of the meat. Prick the leg thoroughly down to the bone with a fork. Except ghee mix all the ingredients including fried ground onions, and apply evenly all over the leg. Prick again so that spices enter the body of the meat. Marinade for two hours. No water to be added.

• Place the leg in a thick bottomed wide open pan with ghee, put on a moderate fire and cover. Put some live charcoals on top of the lid. Turn leg occasionally and baste it with the ghee. Cook till it is absolutely tender.

• Alternatively bake it in a moderately hot oven (300° to 350°F), turning and basting as above, for about 2 hours or till it is well cooked.

Paya Khushk*

Preparation time: 1 hour ● Cooking time: 2 hours ● To serve: 4 – 6 persons.

½ kg. Trotters dressed and cut into 2″ pieces (roughly 4 average trotters)
2 Black cardamoms whole
2 2″ Cinnamon sticks
4 Cloves whole
2 Bay leaves whole
60 gms. Ghee

115 gms. Onions thinly and evenly sliced
12 gms. Salt
15 gms. Red chillies powdered
6 gms. Coriander seeds powdered
6 gms. Kachri powdered
3 gms. Turmeric

3 gms. Cumin seeds whole
25 gms. Garlic ground
1½ gms. *Garam masala* powder
2 tbsps. Fresh coriander leaves chopped.

● Clean the trotters by dipping them in boiling water and scraping away hair and deposits with a knife. Keep on repeating this process till the trotters are absolutely clean. While doing so take care in not cutting away the skin. Cut them into 2″ pieces. Cleaned trotters are also available at most of the butcher shops.

● Boil the trotter pieces in water along with cardamoms, cinnamon, cloves and bay leaves till they are absolutely tender. Alternatively, boil them in pressure cooker with 4 cups of water at 15 lbs. pressure for 45 minutes.

● In a separate pan heat the ghee and fry sliced onions to a golden brown, remove, crush and keep aside.

● In the same ghee add salt, red chillies, coriander seeds, kachri, turmeric, cumin seeds and garlic, and *bhunao* till well-browned. Add trotters along with the water in which the trotters were boiled. Add fried crushed onions and stir. Cook on low fire till the liquid dries up completely. Add *garam masala* powder and fresh coriander leaves.

* Picture on page 52.

Paya ki Nihari

Preparation time: 1 hour • Cooking time: 2 hours • To serve: 4 – 6 persons.

½ kg. Trotters dressed and cut into 2″ pieces (roughly 4 average trotters)
90 gms. Ghee for *masala*
18 gms. Salt
18 gms. Red chillies powdered
25 gms. Coriander seeds powdered

25 gms. Ginger scraped and ground
25 gms. Garlic ground
12 gms. Refined flour (*Maida*)
120 mls. (4 ozs.) Milk
90 gms. Ghee for *baghar*
115 gms. Onions thinly and evenly sliced

10 Cloves powdered
10 Cardamoms powdered
20 Pepper corns powdered
2 2″ Cinnamon sticks
15 mls. (½ oz.) Lime juice.

- Clean the trotters as described in the previous recipe. Boil the trotter pieces in pressure cooker with 4 cups of water at 15 lbs. pressure for 45 minutes.
- Remove the trotters and keep aside. Add garlic into the trotter-liquid and stir and keep it aside to be used in *bhunao*.
- Heat the ghee, add salt, red chillies, coriander seeds and ginger. *Bhunao*, adding a little trotter-liquid (with garlic) at a time, till the liquid is fully used. Add trotter pieces and one cup of water. Dilute refined flour in milk, and add to the trotters. Cook on low fire, stirring regularly till the gravy becomes thick.
- In a separate pan heat the ghee for *baghar* and fry sliced onions to a golden brown. Remove, grind and add to the trotters. In the same ghee, add cloves, cardamoms, pepper corns and cinnamon, and at once add to the trotters and stir. Delay may burn the *masala*. Add lime juice.
- Mainly to be eaten with rice.

Keema Matar

Preparation time: 30 minutes • Cooking time: 1 hour • To serve: 8 – 10 persons.

½ kg. Minced lean mutton from leg *or* shoulder (*Keema*)

30 gms. Salt

25 gms. Red chillies powdered

25 gms. Coriander seeds powdered

6 gms. Turmeric

6 gms. Cumin seeds whole

115 gms. Onions ground

25 gms. Garlic ground

25 gms. Ginger scraped and ground

225 gms. Curd

225 gms. Ghee

750 gms. Green peas fresh and shelled

25 gms. Green chillies finely chopped without seeds

9 gms. Sugar

3 gms. *Garam masala* powder

30 mls. (1 oz.) Lime juice

1 tbsp. Fresh coriander leaves chopped.

• Mix salt, red chillies, coriander seeds, turmeric, cumin seeds, onions, garlic, ginger and curd into the meat and marinade for half an hour.

• Heat the ghee, add marinaded meat and stir. Cook covered. When the liquids dry up, *bhunao* till well-browned. Add four cups of water. When meat is tender and a little water remains, add peas, green chillies and sugar. Reduce the heat and cook till the peas are tender, but not mushy, and water dries up. Add *garam masala* powder, lime juice and coriander leaves and stir.

Keema Hari Mirch ka Do Peeaza

Green chillies were always a weakness with my father. He loved them and developed this unusual recipe. Lovers of slightly hot food would love this Keema.

Preparation time: 45 minutes ● Cooking time: 1 hour ● To serve: 6 – 8 persons.

½ kg. Minced lean mutton from leg *or* shoulder (*Keema*)
115 gms. Curd
25 gms. Salt
6 gms. Turmeric
3 gms. Cumin seeds whole

175 gms. Ghee
115 gms. Onions thinly and evenly sliced
250 gms. Green chillies
115 gms. Onions cut into 1" pieces

50 gms. Garlic whole
30 mls. (1 oz.) Lime juice
2 tbsps. Fresh coriander leaves chopped.

● Slit green chillies and remove seeds. Cut the green chillies into ½" pieces and keep aside.
● Mix thoroughly curd, salt, turmeric and cumin seeds into the meat.
● Heat the ghee and fry sliced onions to a golden brown. Add minced meat and stir. Add about 4 cups of water and cook covered, stirring occasionally. When meat is half-cooked, add green chillies, onion pieces and garlic, and stir. When tender and water dries up, add lime juice and coriander leaves.

Keema Karela

Preparation time: 1 hour • Cooking time: $1\frac{1}{2}$ hours • To serve: 4 – 6 persons.

$\frac{1}{2}$ kg. Bitter gourd (*Karela*) long variety, scraped and seeded

25 gms. Salt for applying on bitter gourd

6 gms. Turmeric for applying on bitter gourd

$\frac{1}{2}$ kg. Minced lean mutton from leg *or* shoulder (*Keema*)

60 gms. Ghee for mutton

115 gms. Onions, thinly and evenly sliced

9 gms. Salt

12 gms. Coriander seeds powdered

3 gms. Cumin seeds powdered

3 gms. Ani seeds powdered

3 gms. *Garam masala* powder

12 gms. Ginger scraped and ground

A pinch of Asafoetida diluted in water

60 gms. Ghee for frying bitter gourds

6 gms. Salt

6 gms. Red chillies powdered

6 gms. Coriander seeds, powdered

250 gms. Curd.

- Scrape bitter gourds. Make a slit lengthwise and discard the seeds.
- Apply thoroughly salt and turmeric over and inside the bitter gourds and keep for an hour. Then press the bitter gourds gently with your palms, squeezing out the liquid completely. Wash them thoroughly in fresh water and squeeze again. Put the bitter gourds in boiling water and cook them for one minute. Remove and squeeze again.
- Heat the ghee and fry bitter gourds to a golden brown. Remove and keep aside.
- In a separate pan heat the ghee and fry sliced onions to a golden brown. Add minced meat and salt and enough water to cook the meat. When tender and very little water remains, add coriander seeds, cumin seeds, ani seeds, *garam masala*, ginger and asafoetida. Simmer on low fire till water dries up completely.
- Stuff bitter gourds with the meat. Tie a piece of thread around bitter gourds to prevent meat from running out.
- In a *kadhai* put ghee in which bitter gourds were fried, and add the remaining ingredients. Add stuffed bitter gourds, cover and simmer on very low fire, stirring occasionally. When the liquids dry up completely and bitter gourds are well-browned, remove the threads.
- Serve hot or cold.

41

Gosht ka Bharta

Preparation time: 30 minutes • Cooking time: 1 hour • To serve: 4 – 6 persons.

½ kg. Minced lean mutton from leg or shoulder (*Keema*)
25 gms. Ghee for mutton
12 gms. Salt
6 gms. Coriander seeds powdered

100 gms. Ghee for frying onions and *masala*
115 gms. Onions thinly and evenly sliced
6 gms. Ginger scraped and chopped finely
115 gms. Curd

8 Cloves powdered
4 Cardamoms powdered
2 2" Cinnamon sticks powdered
6 gms. Pepper corns powdered.

• Cook minced meat in water along with ghee, salt and coriander seeds. When tender, dry the liquids completely. Grind it finely.
• Heat the ghee and fry sliced onions to a golden brown. Remove, grind and keep aside.
• In the same ghee add ground meat and ginger. *Bhunao* it till dark brown. Add fried ground onions and all the remaining ingredients. Stir well. Put on *dum* till the curd dries up completely.
• Can be kept for a week.

42

Kaleji ka Raita*

Preparation time: 30 minutes • Cooking time: 30 minutes • To serve: 6 – 8 persons.

½ kg. Liver
1 kg. Curd fresh and thick
12 gms. Salt

6 gms. Red chillies powdered
12 gms. Mustard powdered

6 gms. Cumin seeds powdered
6 gms. Sugar powdered.

• Boil water. Add whole liver and boil for 15 minutes. Remove and wipe off all the moisture, cut into very thin about 1½″ long and ⅛″ wide strips.
• Remove all the membranes and veins.
• Beat the curd and mix in all the ingredients. Add sliced liver and mix well. Give *dhungar*, method No. 2.
• To be served cold.

Picture on page 52.

Sasranga*

Preparation time: 30 minutes • Cooking time: 1 hour • To serve: 6 – 8 persons.

½ kg. Finely minced lean mutton from leg *or* shoulder (*Keema*)

60 gms. Ghee

30 gms. Almonds blanched and shredded

30 gms. Raisins chopped

60 gms. Onions thinly and evenly sliced

15 gms. Salt

115 gms. *Malai*

50 gms. Green chillies chopped finely with seeds

12 gms. Fresh coriander leaves finely chopped

12 gms. Ginger scraped and finely chopped

15 mls. (½ oz.) Lime juice

4 Eggs lightly beaten.

• Heat the ghee and fry almonds and raisins separately and keep aside.

• In the same ghee fry sliced onions to a golden brown, remove, crush with hand coarsely and keep aside.

• In the same ghee add minced meat with salt and cook. When the meat juices dry up, fry the meat for a minute. Add about 4 cups of water and cook. When the meat is tender, dry the liquids completely.

• In a separate pan mix together almonds, raisins, fried onions, ginger, green chillies and coriander leaves. Mix lime juice in the eggs.

• Grease lightly an 8" round baking dish and put greased paper at its bottom. Spread half of the meat evenly. On top of the meat spread half of the *malai*. Then spread half of the almond mixture. On that sprinkle half of the egg-lime juice mixture, press gently with fingers. Repeat these layers, in the same order, and press again gently with fingers.

• Bake in a moderately hot oven for about 30 minutes, or till it becomes firm. Cool and cut into squares.

• Ideal as a snack.

* *Picture on page 69.*

44

Mokal Bhavnagar

I am grateful to His Highness Maharaja Virbhadrasinghji of Bhavnagar for giving me this fine recipe.

Preparation time: 30 minutes ● Cooking time: 1 hour ● To serve: 6 – 8 persons.

750 gms. Minced lean mutton from leg *or* shoulder (*Keema*)
250 gms. Onions cut into ½" pieces
250 gms. Ghee
½ kg. Onions finely chopped
36 gms. Salt

36 gms. Red chillies powdered
36 gms. Coriander seeds powdered
3 gms. Turmeric
36 gms. Garlic ground
36 gms. Poppy seeds ground with water

75 gms. Coconut grated and ground with water
3 gms. *Garam masala* powder
45 mls.(1½ ozs.) Lime juice
2 tbsps. Fresh coriander leaves chopped.

● Boil together minced meat and onion pieces in about 6 cups of water. When cooked, dry the liquids completely. Pass it through a meat mincer or grind finely.

● Heat the ghee and fry chopped onions to a golden brown. Add salt, red chillies, coriander seeds, turmeric, garlic, poppy seeds and coconut, and *bhunao* till well-browned.

● Add meat and stir well. No water to be added. Cook on low heat stirring all the time to avoid meat sticking to the bottom of the pan. When the meat stops sticking to the bottom and gets crisp, add lime juice, *garam masala* powder and coriander leaves, and stir.

● Can be kept for a week.

● Can be made of chicken or any game meat.

Kofta Sailana*

Preparation time: 1 hour ● Cooking time: 1 hour ● To serve: 6 – 8 persons.

½ kg. Minced lean mutton from leg or shoulder (*Keema*)

25 gms. Ghee for mutton

8 gms. Salt for mutton

6 gms. Red chillies powdered for mutton

36 gms. Parched grams powdered

1 Egg

115 gms. Onions thinly and evenly sliced, fried and ground

250 gms. Curd fresh and thick

36 gms. Almonds blanched, roasted dry and ground with water

12 gms. Charoli roasted dry and ground with water

12 gms. Poppy seeds roasted dry and ground with water

12 gms. Coconut grated, roasted dry and ground with water

1½ gms. Seeds of cardamom powdered

1½ gms. Cinnamon powdered

1½ gms. Black cumin seeds powdered

5 Cloves powdered

A pinch of Saffron diluted in warm water

60 gms. Onions finely chopped

12 gms. Raisins finely chopped

12 gms. Green chillies finely chopped with seeds

1½ gms. Fresh mint leaves finely chopped

8 mls. (¼ oz.) Lime juice

250 gms. Ghee for frying kofta

8 gms. Salt for *masala*

6 gms. Red chillies powdered for *masala*

25 gms. Ginger scraped and ground for *masala*

1 tbsp. Fresh coriander leaves chopped.

● Put the curd in a muslin and hang it on a peg for two hours. Then whip it and keep aside.

● Boil the minced meat along with ghee, salt and red chillies in 4 cups of water. When meat is tender, dry the liquids completely. Grind it finely. Add parched grams and egg. Add half of the fried onions and half of the curd.

● Mix together almonds, charoli, poppy seeds, coconut, cardamoms, cinnamon, black cumin seeds, cloves and saffron. Add two-thirds of this mixture to the meat and knead well. Give *dhungar*, method No. 3. Divide into 16 equal parts.

● For stuffing, mix chopped onions, raisins, green chillies, mint leaves and lime juice, and divide into 16 equal parts. Flatten each part of the meat, put in its centre one part of the stuffing and shape into a ball, wetting hands with a little water to give Koftas a smooth and even shape.

* Picture on page 69.

- Heat the ghee, and fry the Koftas, 5–6 at a time, to a golden brown. Keep aside.
- In the same ghee add salt, red chillies and ginger to the remaining fried onions, the remaining curd and the remaining almond mixture. *Bhunao* till well-browned and ghee separates from the *masala*.
- Add two cups of water. When it starts boiling add the Koftas. Add chopped coriander leaves. Put on *dum* till the Koftas become soft.

46

Kofta Sudarshan

Preparation time: 30 minutes • Cooking time: 1 hour • To serve: 6 – 8 persons.

½ kg. Finely minced lean mutton from leg *or* shoulder (*Keema*)

50 gms. Ghee for mutton

36 gms. Curd

12 gms. Salt

6 gms. Red chillies powdered

6 gms. Coriander seeds powdered

6 gms. Cumin seeds whole

25 gms. Ginger scraped and ground

60 gms. Onions thinly and evenly sliced, fried and ground

15 gms. Green chillies chopped finely without seeds

1 tbsp. Coriander leaves chopped

9 gms. *Garam masala* powder

175 gms. Ghee for gravy

60 gms. Curd

1½ gms. Red chillies powdered

3 gms. Dry ginger powdered.

- Mix thoroughly ghee, curd, salt, red chillies, coriander seeds, cumin seeds, ginger, fried ground onions, green chillies and coriander leaves into the meat. Also half of the *garam masala* powder. Make Koftas rolling each into a sausage shape, about 3" in length, wetting hands with a little water to give Koftas a smooth and even shape.
- Heat the ghee and add curd, well beaten, and keep on stirring till its water dries up and turns dark brown. Add about 4 cups of water and stir. When it starts boiling, add Koftas. Cook uncovered till they become firm. Then cover and cook on medium fire. When they are tender and very little water remains, add remaining half of the *garam masala* powder, red chillies, dry ginger powder. Put on *dum* till water dries up and only ghee remains.

Kofta Saleem

I am grateful to Mallik Saleem Khan Sahib of Dasada (Gujerat) for giving me this fine recipe.

Preparation time: 30 minutes ● Cooking time: 1 hour ● To serve: 6 – 8 persons.

½ kg. Minced lean mutton from leg *or* shoulder (*Keema*)

175 gms. Ghee

250 gms. Onions thinly and evenly sliced

15 gms. Salt

6 gms. Red chillies powdered

6 gms. Cumin seeds powdered

9 gms. *Garam masala* powder

12 gms. Ginger scraped and ground

12 gms. Green chillies chopped finely with seeds

1 tbsp. Fresh leaves of coriander chopped

1½ gms. Cumin seeds whole for *dhungar*

2 Bay leaves

6 gms. Red chillies powdered

175 gms. Curd well beaten.

● Grind the meat finely.

● Heat the ghee and fry sliced onions to a golden brown. Remove and grind dry.

● Add salt, red chillies, cumin seeds, *garam masala* powder, ginger, green chillies and coriander leaves into the meat. Add half of the fried ground onions and mix and knead well. Give *dhungar*, method No. 3, of cumin seeds thrice.

● Make Koftas rolling each into a sausage shape, about 4″ in length, pressing firmly and wetting hands with a little water to give Koftas a smooth and even shape.

● Heat the above ghee and add bay leaves. Add about 4 cups of water. When it starts boiling, add Koftas. Cook uncovered till they become firm. *If covered at early stage the Koftas will break.* Then cover and cook on medium fire. After 15 minutes add curd, red chillies and remaining half of the fried ground onions. Reduce the heat and simmer till the liquids dry up completely and only ghee remains.

Top: Goolar Kabab
Mid-left: Sasranga
Mid-right: Mutton Dahi Bara
Bottom: Kofta Sailana

* Picture on facing page.

Kofta Dilpasand

Preparation time: 30 minutes • Cooking time: 1 hour • To serve: 6 – 8 persons.

Ingredients for Kofta

½ kg. Finely minced lean mutton from leg
  or shoulder (*Keema*)
12 gms. Salt
 9 gms. Red chillies powdered
 9 gms. Coriander seeds powdered
1½ gms. Turmeric

12 gms. Ginger scraped and ground
1½ gms. *Garam masala* powder
60 gms. Curd
25 gms. Ghee
115 gms. Khoa
  A pinch of Asafoetida diluted in water

12 gms. Green chillies finely chopped with seeds
 6 gms. Panjabi badi powdered
 1 tbsp. Fresh coriander leaves chopped.

Ingredients for *Masala*

175 gms. Ghee
115 gms. Curd
 6 gms. Salt
 6 gms. Red chillies powdered
12 gms. Coriander seeds powdered

1½ gms. Turmeric
12 gms. Ginger scraped and ground
  A pinch of Asafoetida diluted in water

1½ gms. *Garam masala* powder
  A pinch of Saffron diluted in warm water.

● Mix thoroughly all the ingredients for the Koftas into the meat. Make Koftas, rolling each into a sausage shape about 3" in length, pressing the mince firmly, wetting hands with a little water to give Koftas a smooth and even shape.

● Heat the ghee and add curd, salt, red chillies, coriander seeds, turmeric and ginger. Fry till *masala* becomes light brown. Add about 4 cups of water and stir. When it starts boiling add Koftas. Cook them uncovered till they become firm. Add asafoetida. Then cover and cook on medium heat till they are tender and very little water remains. Add *garam masala* and saffron. Put on *dum* till water dries up and only ghee remains.

Top: Kabab-e-Murgh
Left: Sabj Murgh
Bottom: Murgh Irani

Kofta Narma Dil

Koftas are cooked in every house, but these are unusual in their softness. As the name suggests they are like a soft or kind heart.

Preparation time: 30 minutes • Cooking time: 1 hour • To serve: 6 – 8 persons.

Ingredients for Kofta

½ kg. Minced lean mutton from leg *or* shoulder (*Keema*)
115 gms. Split grams

6 gms. Salt
12 gms. Red chillies powdered
60 gms. Onions ground

6 gms. *Garam masala* powder
White of a large egg

Ingredients for Stuffing

60 gms. Onions finely chopped
12 gms. Ginger scraped and finely chopped

12 gms. Green chillies finely chopped with seeds

3 gms. Fresh mint leaves finely chopped

Ingredients for Gravy

250 gms. Ghee
3 gms. Cardamoms whole
12 gms. Salt
12 gms. Red chillies powdered

30 gms. Coriander seeds powdered
30 gms. Onions ground
12 gms. Garlic ground

12 gms. Ginger scraped and ground
60 gms. Curd.

• Boil minced meat along with split grams, salt, red chillies and onions in about 4 cups of water. When meat is tender, dry the liquids completely. Grind it finely. Add *garam masala* powder and white of an egg, mix and knead well. Divide into 16 equal parts.

• For stuffing, in a separate pan, mix chopped onions, ginger, green chillies and mint leaves. Divide into 16 equal parts.

• Flatten each part of the meat, put in its centre one part of the stuffing and shape into a ball, wetting hands with a little water to give Koftas a smooth and even shape.

• Heat the ghee and fry the Koftas 5–6 at a time to a golden brown. Keep aside. In the same ghee add cardamoms whole, when they turn black, remove and discard. In the same ghee add the remaining ingredients and *bhunao* them till well-browned and ghee separates from the *masala*. Add one cup of water, when it starts boiling, add Koftas. Put on *dum* till ghee floats on top of the gravy.

Chui Mui ke Kofte
(Kofta Touch Me Not)

Even softer than Kofta Narma Dil, I call these Koftas 'Touch me not'. They maintain shape only as long as they are not touched.

Preparation time: 30 minutes ● Cooking time: 1 hour ● To serve: 6 – 8 persons.

Ingredients for Kofta

- ½ kg. Minced lean mutton from leg *or* shoulder (*Keema*)
- 6 gms. Salt
- 3 gms. Red chillies powdered
- 12 gms. Coriander seeds powdered
- 50 gms. Onions ground
- 6 gms. Garlic ground
- 60 gms. Curd fresh and thick
- 60 gms. Onions thinly and evenly sliced, fried and ground dry.

Ingredients for Gravy

- 250 gms. Ghee
- 6 gms. Salt
- 3 gms. Red chillies powdered
- 12 gms. Coriander seeds powdered
- 60 gms. Onions ground
- 25 gms. Ginger scraped and ground
- 6 gms. Almonds blanched and ground with water
- 3 gms. Charoli ground with water
- 3 gms. Poppy seeds ground with water
- 3 gms. Coconut grated and ground with water
- 3 gms. *Garam masala* powder.

● Boil minced meat along with salt, red chillies, coriander seeds, onions and garlic in about 4 cups of water. When meat is tender, dry the liquids completely. Grind it finely. Add curd and fried ground onions. Make 16 Koftas, round balls, wetting hands with a little water to give the Koftas a smooth and even shape.

● Heat the ghee. Add all the remaining ingredients and *bhunao* till well-browned and ghee separates from the *masala*. Add half cup of water. When it starts boiling, add the Koftas gently. Do not stir with spoon. Keep on shaking the pan gently with hands. As soon as the water dries up, remove the pan from fire and serve at once in a shallow dish.

● Koftas should be added just before serving.

51

Nargisi Kofta

Preparation time: 30 minutes • Cooking time: 1½ hours • To serve: 6 – 8 persons.

Ingredients for Kofta

½ kg. Minced lean mutton from leg *or* shoulder (*Keema*)

6 gms. Salt

3 gms. Red chillies powdered

3 gms. Coriander seeds powdered

1½ gms. *Garam masala* powder

1 Egg

8 Eggs hard–boiled and shelled

A little refined flour for coating eggs.

Ingredients for Gravy

115 gms. Ghee

60 gms. Onions thinly and evenly sliced

9 gms. Salt

9 gms. Red chillies powdered

9 gms. Coriander seeds powdered

25 gms. Garlic ground

115 gms. Curd

50 gms. Coconut grated and ground with water

2 Bay leaves whole

1½ gms. *Garam masala* powder

30 mls. (1 oz.) Kewada water

A pinch of Saffron diluted in warm water.

• Boil minced meat along with salt, red chillies and coriander seeds in about 4 cups of water.. When meat is tender, dry the liquids completely. Grind it finely. Add *garam masala* powder and eggs, mix and knead well. If necessary, add a little water in the meat to make it pliable. Divide into 8 equal parts. Flatten.

• Roll the eggs lightly in flour. Fold the meat evenly and smoothly round the floured eggs, wetting hands with a little water to give Koftas a smooth and even shape.

• Heat the ghee in a frying pan. Fry the Koftas to a dark brown. Cool and halve each Kofta with a sharp knife dipped in hot water. Keep aside.

• In the same ghee fry, sliced onions to a golden brown. Add salt, red chillies, coriander seeds, garlic and curd, and *bhunao* till well-browned and ghee separates from *masala*. Add the remaining ingredients and 1 cup of water and stir. Pour the above gravy in a heat-proof serving dish and arrange the Koftas on top of the gravy. Do not stir.

• Simmer on low heat till the liquids dry up and only ghee remains.

Goolar Kabab*

'Goolar' is the Indian wild fig. As the name of this recipe suggests these Kababs resemble the Goolar fruit.

Preparation time: 30 minutes • Cooking time: 2 hours • To serve: 8 – 10 persons.

½ kg. Minced lean mutton from leg *or* shoulder (*Keema*)

115 gms. Split grams (*Chana dal*)

12 gms. Salt

3 gms. Red chillies powdered

30 gms. Onions ground

6 gms. Ginger scraped and ground

60 gms. Curd

6 gms. *Garam masala* powder

60 gms. Onions finely chopped

12 gms. Green chillies finely chopped with seeds

6 gms. Fresh mint leaves finely chopped

8 mls. (¼ oz.) Lime juice *or* vinegar

1 Egg lightly beaten Poppy seeds whole for coating the Kababs

Ghee for frying the Kababs.

● Boil the minced meat along with split grams, salt, red chillies, onions and ginger in 8 cups of water for one hour. When meat is tender, dry the liquids completely. Grind it very finely. Add curd and *garam masala* powder, mix and knead well.

● Divide into 20 equal parts.

● For stuffing, mix chopped onions, green chillies, mint leaves and lime juice and divide into 20 equal parts.

● Flatten each part of the meat, put in its centre one part of the stuffing and shape into a ball, wetting hands with a little water to give Kababs a smooth and even shape. Dip the Kababs into the egg and roll in poppy seeds to give an even coating.

● Heat the ghee in a frying pan and deep fry the Kababs, 6–7 at a time, on medium heat till golden brown.

* *Picture on page 69.*

53

Shikampuri Kabab

I am grateful to His late Highness Maharajadhiraj Hari Singhji of Kashmir for giving this fine recipe.

Preparation time: 30 minutes • Cooking time: 2 hours • To serve: 6 – 8 persons.

1½ kg. Finely minced lean mutton from leg *or* shoulder (*Keema*)

36 gms. Split grams (*Chana dal*)

36 gms. Salt

6 gms. Red chillies whole

36 gms. Green chillies whole

6 Black cardamoms whole

6 Bay leaves whole

6 1" Cinnamon sticks whole

12 Cloves whole

115 gms. Curd

6 gms. *Garam masala* powder

75 gms. Green chillies finely chopped with seeds

36 gms. Fresh coriander leaves finely chopped

45 mls. (1½ oz.) Lime juice

½ kg. *Malai*

3 Eggs lightly beaten Ghee for frying Kababs.

• Keep *malai* in a refrigerator for 8 to 10 hours or till it is firm. Take it out just before using it for filling. This is important as otherwise it will be difficult to shape the Kababs with soft *malai*.

• Boil meat along with split grams, salt, red chillies, green chillies, black cardamoms, bay leaves, cinnamon and cloves in about 8 cups of water. Boil for an hour and dry the water completely. No moisture should remain. Discard red chillies, green chillies and *garam masala*. Grind the meat very finely. Add curd, eggs, *garam masala* powder, chopped green chillies, coriander leaves and lime juice to the meat and mix and knead well. Divide meat and *malai*, separately, into 18 equal parts. Into meat fill *malai* and shape into sausage like form 4" long, wetting hands with a little water to give Kababs a smooth and even shape. Heat the ghee in a frying pan and deep fry Kababs, three at a time, on medium heat to a golden brown.

Mutton Dahi Bara*

In his quest for the unusual, my father wondered why Dahi Baras could not be made of meat. After some experimentation he perfected this superb combination.

Preparation time: 30 minutes • Cooking time: 1½ hours • To serve: 10 persons.

½ kg. Minced lean mutton from leg *or* shoulder (*Keema*)
12 gms. Salt
12 gms. Red chillies powdered
12 gms. Coriander seeds powdered
3 gms. Turmeric
3 gms. Cumin seeds whole

100 gms. Onions ground
12 gms. Garlic ground
12 gms. Ginger scraped and ground
60 gms. Split grams (*Chana dal*)
6 gms. *Garam masala* powder
750 gms. Curd fresh and thick

6 gms. Salt
18 gms. Sugar powdered
4 gms. Fresh mint leaves finely chopped
600 mls. Sour buttermilk
Ghee for frying baras.

• Boil meat in about 4 cups of water along with salt, red chillies, coriander seeds, turmeric, cumin seeds, onions, garlic, ginger and split grams. When tender dry the liquids completely. Add *garam masala* powder. Grind the meat finely.

• Divide into 20 equal parts. Flatten, wetting hands with a little water to give baras a smooth and even shape.

• Heat the ghee in a frying pan and shallow fry the baras, a few at a time, to dark brown in colour. Immediately, put them in buttermilk. When they sink in the bottom, take out and with both hands squeeze each of them gently to remove superfluous fat and water, taking care not to break them. Put them in a serving dish.

• Sieve curd through a muslin and mix into it salt, sugar and mint leaves. Pour curd on baras and let them stand about an hour. Serve cold.

• Not to be put in refrigerator as they lose their softness.

* *Picture on page 69.*

Sabj Murgh*

Preparation time: 45 minutes ● Cooking time: 1½ hours ● To serve: 4 – 6 persons.

½ kg. Chicken dressed
6 gms. Ginger scraped and ground
6 gms. Garlic ground
175 gms. Ghee
30 gms. Almonds blanched and cut into thick slices

15 gms. Raisins cut into halves
12 gms. Salt
250 gms. Curd
115 gms. Khoa ground
60 gms. Green chillies whole

115 gms. Fresh coriander leaves chopped
115 gms. Green coconut for extracting milk.

● Remove the skin of the chicken. Cut into pieces. Add ginger and garlic to the chicken and marinade for 30 minutes.

● Prick the green chillies with a fork and keep aside. For extracting coconut milk, first grate the coconut, then grind it finely adding 1 cup of hot water, a little at a time. Squeeze through a muslin. Repeat the process to take out milk to the maximum.

● Heat the ghee and fry sliced almonds and raisins separately to a golden colour and keep aside. In the same ghee add the chicken and fry it to a golden brown. Add salt, curd and khoa. Cook till the curd dries up. Add green chillies and coriander leaves, and stir. Add coconut milk and cook on low fire, stirring regularly. No water to be added. When tender, add almonds and raisins. Put on *dum*. Remove from fire as soon as the liquids dry up.

* *Picture on page 70.*

56

Kabab Murgh Shirin (Sweet)*

Preparation time: 30 minutes • Cooking time: 2 hours • To serve: 6 – 8 persons.

½ kg. Chicken skinned and boned
1 litre Milk
115 gms. Khoa
1 Egg
50 gms. Almonds blanched and chopped

50 gms. Charoli blanched and chopped
50 gms. Raisins chopped
½ kg. Sugar

A good pinch of Saffron, diluted in warm water
30 mls. (1 oz.) Kewada water
Ghee for frying the Kababs.

● Mince the chicken and boil it in milk. When tender, dry the milk completely. Grind chicken finely. Add khoa and egg to the chicken and mix well. Divide into 16 equal parts.

● For stuffing mix almonds, charoli and raisins and divide into 16 equal parts.

● Flatten each part of the chicken. Put in its centre one part of the stuffing and shape into a ball, flatten again, wetting hands with a little water to give kababs a smooth and even shape.

● Heat the ghee in a frying pan and deep fry the kababs, a few at a time, to a dark brown.

● In a separate pan put sugar and 4 cups of water. Cook, stirring till syrup gets one-thread consistency. Add saffron and kewada water.

● Put kababs into the syrup. Put on fire. When it starts boiling remove from fire.

● Serve hot or cold.

Picture on page 87.

Murgh Kabab Gorkhar*

Preparation time: 1 hour ● Cooking time: 2 hours ● To serve: 4 – 6 persons.

1 Chicken whole weighing 500 gms. to 600 gms. dressed and skinned
6 gms. Salt
60 gms. Onions chopped finely
30 gms. Fresh coriander leaves chopped finely

25 gms. Green chillies chopped finely with seeds
3 gms. Cinnamon powdered
20 Cloves powdered
40 Pepper corns powdered

3 gms. Cardamoms (*Ilachi*) powdered
15 mls. (½ oz.) Lime juice
115 gms. Curd fresh and thick
6 gms. Salt.

● Preferably, dress the chicken 12 hours before cooking it. Remove the skin. Cut out the oil sac, that little protuberance at the tip of the tail. Clean, wash and dry well. With a string tie neck, wings and legs close to the body. This will be otherwise difficult once the body of the chicken gets stiff.

● Mix together salt, onions, coriander leaves and green chillies. Add half the quantity of cinnamon, cloves, pepper corns and cardamoms. Mix well.

● Fill the above mixture in the chicken. Close the cavity by placing tooth picks across and lacing together with a string.

● Mix the remaining ingredients and remaining half of cinnamon, cloves, pepper corns and cardamoms. Mix well. Apply all over the chicken and marinade it, preferably in sunlight, for half an hour.

● Put the chicken, breast side down, in a pre-heated oven and bake it on a medium heat. Keep on turning the side of the chicken occasionally. Cook till it is tender, and well-browned.

● While serving cut it into large pieces.

* Picture on page 87.

Murgh ka Soola

Preparation time: 1 hour • Cooking time: 2 hours • To serve: 4 – 6 persons.

½ kg. Large pieces of young chicken
Raw papaya peeled and finely ground enough to cover the chicken pieces
15 gms. Salt
12 gms. Red chillies powdered
25 gms. Khoa

12 gms. Almonds blanched, fried and ground with water
60 gms. Onions sliced, fried and ground with water
12 gms. Garlic chopped, fried and ground with water
6 gms. Ginger scraped and ground

3 gms. Parched grams powdered
1½ gms. *Garam masala* powder
60 gms. Curd sour
60 gms. Ghee, preferably pure.

• Remove the skin of the chicken. Cut out the oil sac, that little protuberance at the tip of the tail. Cut into large pieces. Wash and dry with a cloth. Prick the pieces well with a fork. Wrap ground papaya all over the pieces and marinade for 12 hours. Then wipe off the papaya. Do not wash the pieces.

• Mix well all the ingredients, except ghee, and apply all over the chicken pieces.

• Take a skewer, preferably two-pronged, about 18" long. Pass the skewer through the pieces. Pack the pieces closely, levelling the *masala* in between the pieces. With a string tie the pieces, first from one end of the skewer to the other end and then around the pieces to keep them firm while cooking.

• Light a layer of charcoal and let them burn until white ash appears on the surface. Rest the skewer on some platform, at both sides of the fire, so that the chicken pieces remain 6" above the fire. Keep on rotating the skewer to cook evenly. Cook on low fire till chicken is tender. Then increase the fire to medium, and baste chicken with ghee, a little at a time till all the ghee finishes and chicken is well-browned.

• Remove the strings. Gently take out chicken into a pan. Give *dhungar*, method No. 3 of cloves. Close the pan and put on *dum* for an hour.

• Partridges and quails can be cooked with the same method.

Kabab-e-Murgh*

Preparation time: 45 minutes ● Cooking time: 3 hours ● To serve: 6 – 8 persons.

1 Chicken whole weighing about 1 kg. dressed and skinned
12 gms. Salt
12 gms. Coriander seeds powdered
12 gms. *Garam masala* powder
12 gms. Ginger scraped and ground
60 gms. Onions ground
A pinch of Saffron diluted in warm water

250 gms. Minced lean mutton from leg *or* shoulder (*Keema*)
60 gms. Ghee
60 gms. Onions thinly and evenly sliced
9 gms. Salt for mutton
9 gms. Coriander seeds powdered for mutton
9 gms. Ginger scraped and ground for mutton
12 gms. Cinnamon sticks whole

12 Wooden sticks about 6" long and of pencil thickness.
One earthen pot with lid, big enough to accommodate the chicken
115 gms. Split black beans (*Urad dal*) flour
20 Cow dung cakes for fire.

● Preferably, dress the chicken 12 hours before cooking it. Remove the skin. Cut out the oil sac, that little protuberance at the tip of the tail. Clean, wash and dry well. With a string tie neck, wings and legs close to the body. This will be otherwise difficult once the body of the chicken gets stiff.

● Mix salt, coriander seeds powder, *garam masala* powder, ginger, onions and saffron, and apply all over the chicken. Keep it in sunlight for about half an hour to dry.

● Heat the ghee and fry sliced onions to a golden brown. Add minced meat along with salt, coriander seeds and ginger. *Bhunao* till well-browned. Add about 4 cups of water and cook. When cooked, dry liquids completely.

● Fill the above minced meat in the chicken. Close the cavity by placing tooth picks across and lacing together with a string. Wash the earthen pot with water. Spread cinnamon sticks in the bottom of the pot. Arrange the wooden sticks, crosswise, in the pot in such a way that the chicken should not touch the bottom or sides of the pot. Put chicken over sticks. Close the pot with the lid. Prepare thick paste of black beans flour by adding water. Seal the edges of the lid with the above paste.

● Dig a round pit, about 18" deep and 18" wide, in a dry ground. Light the cow dung cakes and let them burn until white ash appears on the

* Picture on page 70.

surface. Break them coarsely. Put one-fourth of them in the bottom of the pit spreading evenly. Put on them the sealed earthen pot. Cover the pot from all sides as well as the top with cow dung fire. Level the surface and press it a little.

- After two hours take out the pot and unseal the lid. Take out the chicken, remove the strings and serve.
- Alternatively, spread cinnamon sticks in a baking pan. Put chicken and bake it in a pre-heated oven on medium heat. Keep on turning the sides of the chicken. When tender discard cinnamon sticks, remove the string and serve.

60

Murgh Mumtaz Mahal

Preparation time: 30 minutes • Cooking time: 1½ hours • To serve: 4 – 6 persons.

½ kg. Chicken large pieces	6 gms. Coriander seeds powdered	1½ gms. Seeds of cardamom powdered
150 gms. Ghee	3 gms. Cumin seeds whole	15 mls. (½ oz.) Kewada water
60 gms. Onions thinly and evenly sliced	12 gms. Salt	15 mls. (½ oz.) Lime juice
12 gms. Ginger scraped and shredded	115 gms. Curd	A pinch of Saffron diluted in warm water.
25 gms. Khoa	25 gms. Cashewnuts ground with water	
6 gms. Red chillies powdered		

- Remove the skin of the chicken. Cut out the oil sac, that little protuberance at the tip of the tail. Wash and cut into pieces. Prick the pieces well with a fork.
- Heat the ghee and fry sliced onions to a golden brown. Remove, crush them coarsely and keep aside. In the same ghee fry shredded ginger to a golden brown. Remove, crush them coarsely and keep aside.
- In the same ghee add chicken pieces along with khoa, red chillies, coriander seeds, cumin seeds. Add enough water to cook the chicken. When half-cooked, add salt and curd. When tender and very little liquids remain, add the remaining ingredients. Put on *dum*, till the liquids dry up completely and only ghee remains. Add fried onions and ginger.

Murgh Musallam
Do Rukha Seekh Par

"Do Rukha" means of two tastes. The chicken tastes different from the stuffing. Yet both combine to make this an excellent whole chicken recipe, both decorative and tasty, ideal for parties.

Preparation time: 1 hour • Cooking time: 2 hours • To serve: 4 – 6 persons.

1 Young chicken whole weighing 500 gms. to 600 gms. dressed and skinned
Raw papaya peeled and finely ground enough to cover the whole chicken
115 gms. Finely minced lean mutton from leg *or* shoulder (*Keema*)
30 gms. Ghee for mutton
30 gms. Curd
6 gms. Red chillies powdered
6 gms. Salt

3 gms. Coriander seeds powdered
1½ gms. Cumin seeds
15 gms. Onions ground
6 gms. Garlic ground
1½ gms. *Garam masala* powder
15 mls. (½ oz.) Fresh lime juice
4 Hard boiled eggs shelled and coarsely chopped
15 gms. Almonds blanched and coarsely chopped
15 gms. Raisins (*Kismish*) coarsely chopped
15 gms. Coconut grated

25 gms. Green chillies finely chopped with seeds
6 gms. Ginger scraped and finely chopped
1½ gms. Fresh mint leaves finely chopped
30 gms. Ghee (preferably pure) for chicken
60 gms. Onions finely and evenly sliced
115 gms. Curd
25 gms. Parched grams powdered
6 gms. Salt.

• Prepare the chicken as described in Recipe No. 59. Prick the chicken well with a fork. Wrap ground papaya all over the chicken and marinade for 12 hours. Then wipe the papaya off and discard. Do not wash the chicken.

• Heat the ghee and add minced meat along with curd, red chillies, salt, coriander seeds, cumin seeds, onions and garlic. *Bhunao* till meat is well-browned. Then add about 4 cups of water and cook till meat is tender and water dries up completely. Add *garam masala* and fresh lime juice. Add eggs, almonds, raisins, coconut, green chillies, ginger and mint leaves to the meat and gently stir.

• In a separate pan heat the ghee and fry sliced onions to a golden brown. Remove from the ghee and crush them coarsely. Keep the ghee aside for later use. Add fried onions to the meat.

• Fill the meat in the chicken. Close the cavity by placing tooth picks across and lacing together with a string. Tie neck, wings and legs close to the body with a string.

● Put the curd in a muslin and hang it on a peg for two hours. (This should be done quite in advance to keep it ready for use). In the curd mix parched grams and salt and apply all over the chicken.

● Take a skewer (seekh) about 18" long (length according to the number of birds). Pass the skewer through the chicken, lengthwise, and tie the chicken with a string to keep it firm while cooking.

● Light a layer of charcoals and let them burn until white ash appears on the surface. Keep the heat low throughout cooking. Rest the skewer on some platform, at both ends of the fire, so that chicken remains 6" above the fire. Keep rotating the skewer to cook evenly. Baste the chicken occasionally with the ghee (in which onions were browned), a little at a time, till all the ghee finishes. Cook for about an hour. When it is nicely tender take it out from the skewer and remove the strings.

62

Murgh Irani*

Preparation time: 30 minutes ● Cooking time: 1½ hours ● To serve: 6 – 8 persons.

½ kg. Chicken, young, cut into pieces
175 gms. Ghee
60 gms. Onions finely and evenly sliced
12 gms. Salt
6 gms. Red chillies powdered
1½ gms. Seeds of cardamom powdered

115 gms. Curd well beaten
60 gms. Onions finely chopped
12 gms. Ginger scraped and ground
12 gms. Garlic finely chopped
60 gms. Almonds blanched and shredded

115 gms. *Malai*
15 mls. (½ oz.) Lime juice
15 mls. (½ oz.) Kewada water
A pinch of Saffron diluted in warm water.

● Remove the skin of the chicken. Cut out the oil sac, that little protuberance at the tip of the tail. Wash and cut into pieces. Prick the pieces well with a fork.

● Heat the ghee and fry sliced onions to a golden brown. Add chicken pieces along with all the ingredients, stir. No water to be added. Cover tightly and cook on very low fire.

● When tender and only ghee remains, remove from the fire, serve when it is almost cold.

* Picture on page 70.

Murgh Musallam Sailana*

Preparation time: 1 hour • Cooking time: $1\frac{1}{2}$ hours • To serve: 4 – 6 persons.

1 Chicken whole weighing 500 gms. to 600 gms. dressed and skinned	$1\frac{1}{2}$ gms. Mace whole	6 gms. Coriander seeds powdered
25 gms. Ghee for frying *masala*	60 gms. Onions thinly and evenly sliced	6 gms. Salt
4 Cloves whole	12 gms. Ginger scraped and ground	12 gms. Almonds blanched and chopped
2 2" Cinnamon sticks whole	12 gms. Cashewnuts ground with water	12 gms. Raisins chopped
2 Black cardamoms whole	25 gms. Poppy seeds ground with water	90 gms. Ghee for chicken
2 Bay leaves	25 gms. Coconut grated and ground with water	6 gms. Salt
		240 mls. (8 ozs.) Milk
		60 gms. Curd.

• Prepare the chicken as described in Recipe No. 59. Heat the ghee and fry separately cloves, cinnamon, black cardamoms, bay leaves and mace lightly. Grind them together with water and keep aside.

• In the same ghee fry sliced onions to a golden brown. Remove, crush coarsely and keep aside.

• In the same ghee add ginger, cashewnuts, poppy seeds, coconut, coriander seeds and salt, and brown them lightly. Add chopped almonds and raisins. Add to it the above fried ground *garam masala* and fried crushed onions. Mix well.

• Fill the above mixture in the chicken. (If the stuffing is in excess keep it aside to be used later on.) Close the cavity by placing tooth picks across and lacing together with a string.

• Heat the ghee. Add chicken and fry till golden brown. Add salt and milk, and enough water to cook it. Cook covered on a medium fire. When tender and very little liquids remain, add curd. Excess stuffing, if any, should be added also. Reduce the heat to the minimum. Put on *dum* till the gravy thickens and ghee films on the surface of the gravy.

Top: Murgh Musallam Sailana
Right: Kabab Murgh Shirin (Sweet)
Bottom: Murgh Kabab Gorkhar

* *Picture on facing page.*

Mahi Ab-e-Hayat*

Preparation time: 1 hour • Cooking time: 1 hour • To serve: 4 – 6 persons.

1 kg. Fish pieces. Any firm white fish

350 gms. Ghee

250 gms. Onions thinly and evenly sliced

25 gms. Coriander seeds powdered

1½ gms. Cinnamon powdered

1½ gms. Cloves powdered

1½ gms. Cardamoms powdered

3 gms. Pepper corns powdered

1½ gms. Ani seeds powdered

115 gms. Finely minced lean mutton from leg or shoulder (*Keema*)

60 gms. Split green beans (*Moong dal*) skinless powdered dry

60 gms. Gram flour (*Besan*)

60 gms. Poppy seeds whole

2 Eggs (white)

25 gms. Ginger scraped, ground and juice extracted

115 gms. Curd.

• Skin the fish, remove bones and cut into pieces. Wash thoroughly, and dry completely on paper or cloth.

• Heat the ghee and fry sliced onions to a golden brown. Remove half of the ghee and keep aside, to be used later on. In the remaining ghee, with fried onions, add fish with salt and coriander seeds and cook. No water to be used. When cooked add cinnamon, cloves, cardamom, pepper corns, and ani seeds. Stir and keep aside.

• In a separate pan put minced meat along with all the remaining ingredients and mix thoroughly. Add this mixture to the fish. Cook on low fire, stirring regularly, till liquid dries up. Reheat the ghee, which was kept aside, and add to the fish, and stir. Simmer on low fire till the mixture stops sticking to the bottom of the pan. When ready, it will look like "Halwa".

Above: Mahi Ab-e-Hayat
Below: Dahi Machchhi

* *Picture on facing page.*

65

Dahi Machchhi*

Preparation time: 1 hour • Cooking time: 1 hour • To serve: 4 – 6 persons.

½ kg. Fish pieces. Any firm white fish
30 gms. Mustard yellow variety (*Sarson*)

12 gms. Salt
12 gms. Green chillies ground with water
3 gms. Turmeric

60 gms. Mustard oil
½ kg. Curd fresh and thick.

• Skin the fish, remove bones and cut into 2″×2″ pieces. Wash well and dry completely on paper or cloth.

• Put the curd in muslin and hang it on a peg for 3 to 4 hours. It should be 250 gms. after draining. Then whip it and keep aside.

• Grind mustard with water and mix in salt and green chillies and keep it for two hours.

• In the curd add mustard, salt, green chillies and turmeric, and stir well. Add fish and stir. Add mustard oil. Put into a pan with tightly fitted lid, and close it. Put this pan, containing fish, into a bigger pan with water coming upto a little less than half the depth of the inner pan. Boil (steam cook) it for an hour. If required add more water during the cooking.

• Take out the pan, open the lid and stir the fish gently.

* *Picture on page 88.*

Machchhi-Methi

Preparation time: 1 hour ● Cooking time: 30 minutes ● To serve: 4 – 6 persons.

½ kg. Fish pieces. Any firm white fish
115 gms. Ghee
3 gms. Fenugreek seeds whole
115 gms. Curd
12 gms. Salt
12 gms. Red chillies powdered

6 gms. Coriander seeds powdered
3 gms. Cumin seeds whole
3 gms. Turmeric
60 gms. Onions ground
25 gms. Garlic ground
12 gms. Ginger scraped and ground

12 gms. Fresh fenugreek leaves chopped
or
3 gms. Dry fenugreek leaves crushed.

● Skin the fish and cut into 2″×2″ pieces. Wash thoroughly and dry completely on paper or cloth.
● Heat the ghee. Add fenugreek seeds. When they turn black, remove and discard.
● In the same ghee add all the remaining ingredients and *bhunao* until well-browned and ghee separates from *masala*.
● Add fish pieces and stir. No water to be added. Cook, uncovered, on medium fire, stirring occasionally and gently not to break the pieces. Cook till the fish is tender and only ghee remains.

Machchhi Dampukh

I am grateful to Her Highness Maharani Lok Rajya Lakshmi of Jhabua for giving me this fine recipe.

Preparation time: 1 hour ● Cooking time: 1 hour ● To serve: 4 – 6 persons.

½ kg. Fish pieces. Any firm white fish
18 gms. Mustard yellow variety (*Sarson*)
9 gms. Salt
3 gms. Red chillies powdered
1½ gms. Turmeric
1½ gms. Cumin seeds powdered

3 gms. Coriander seeds powdered
2 Cloves powdered
2 Cardamoms powdered
1 2" Cinnamon stick powdered
20 Pepper corns powdered
6 gms. Ginger scraped and ground

6 gms. Garlic ground
100 gms. Mustard oil
115 gms. Tomatoes large red cut into thick round slices
60 gms. Onions large cut into thick round slices.

● Skin the fish, remove bones and cut into 2"×2" pieces. Wash thoroughly and dry completely on paper or cloth.
● Grind mustard with water and mix in salt. Keep it for 12 hours before using.
● Add mustard, salt, red chillies, turmeric, cumin seeds, coriander seeds, cloves, cardamoms, cinnamon, pepper corns, ginger and garlic to the fish and mix thoroughly.
● In a 10" wide baking pan put a layer of tomato and onion slices alternatively. Put fish evenly on them. Add mustard oil. Do not stir.
● In a pre-heated oven bake the fish on medium heat for an hour or till the liquids dry up completely and fish is well-browned.
● Serve it in the same pan in which it is baked.

Mahi Be-Nazeer

Preparation time: 1 hour • Cooking time: 30 minutes • To serve: 4 – 6 persons.

½ kg. Fish pieces. Any firm white fish
30 gms. *Malai*
30 gms. Almonds blanched and ground with water
60 gms. Curd fresh and thick
12 gms. Salt
120 gms. Ghee

60 gms. Onions thinly and evenly sliced
12 gms. Red chillies powdered
12 gms. Coriander seeds powdered
18 gms. Ginger scraped and ground
12 gms. Garlic ground

1½ gms. Cumin seeds powdered
4 gms. Cardamoms powdered
4 Cloves powdered
1 2″ Cinnamon stick powdered
15 mls. (½ oz.) Kewada water.

● Skin the fish and cut into 2″×2″ pieces. Wash thoroughly and dry completely on paper or cloth.

● Add *malai*, almonds, curd and salt to the fish, and mix well. Marinade for half an hour.

● Heat the ghee and fry sliced onions to a golden brown. Remove, grind and keep aside.

● In the same ghee add red chillies, coriander seeds, ginger and garlic, and *bhunao* twice.

● Add fish, fried ground onions and stir well. Cook on medium heat, uncovered. Do not add water. Stir occasionally and gently not to break the pieces. When cooked, add all the remaining ingredients and stir gently. Simmer on low heat till ghee films the surface of the gravy.

69

Mahi Kabab Kalia*

Preparation time: 1 hour • Cooking time: 1½ hours • To serve: 6 – 8 persons.

½ kg. Fish pieces
6 gms. Salt for fish
12 gms. Red chillies powdered
3 gms. Cumin seeds powdered
3 gms. Ani seeds roasted dry and powdered
1½ gms. *Garam masala* powder for fish
60 gms. Onions ground

25 gms. Refined flour (*Maida*)
1 Large egg
60 gms. Curd fresh and thick
25 gms. Almonds blanched and ground with water
6 gms. Rice roasted dry and powdered
6 gms. Salt for gravy
12 gms. Coriander seeds powdered

1½ gms. *Garam masala* powder for gravy
6 gms. Ginger scraped and ground
15 mls. (½ oz.) Rose water
1 cup Water
115 gms. Ghee for *baghar*
1½ gms. Cardamoms whole.

• Skin the fish, remove bones and cut into pieces. Put the fish in a colander or sieve. Place the colander on a pan containing only as much water that it should not come upto the colander while boiling. Cover and steam cook till tender. Remove and mash it thoroughly with hand. Add salt, red chillies, cumin seeds, ani seeds, *garam masala* powder, onions, refined flour and egg. Divide into 16 equal parts. Flatten, wetting hands with a little water to give the kababs a smooth and even shape. Grease the colander and steam cook the kababs till firm. (Method is same as given above.) Remove and keep aside.

• In a separate pan put curd, almonds, rose water, rice powder, salt, coriander seeds, *garam masala* powder, ginger and water, and mix thoroughly. Put the pan on fire and keep on stirring till it starts boiling. Remove from fire. Add kababs.

• In a separate pan heat the ghee for *baghar*. Add cardamoms. When they turn dark brown, put the ghee with cardamoms into the fish and stir.

• Put on *dum* till the kababs become tender and ghee films on the surface of the gravy.

* Picture on page 106.

Machchhi ka Soola*

Preparation time: 1 hour • Cooking time: 30 minutes • To serve: 4 – 6 persons.

½ kg. Fish pieces. Any firm white fish
50 gms. Ghee
60 gms. Onions thinly and evenly sliced
25 gms. Garlic chopped
15 gms. Salt

15 gms. Red chillies powdered
9 gms. Coriander seeds powdered
3 gms. Cumin seeds whole
3 gms. Turmeric

12 gms. *Kachri* ground with water
1 tbsp. Fresh coriander leaves chopped
30 mls. (1 oz.) cold water
50 gms. Ghee, preferably pure, for basting.

• Skin the fish, remove bones, and cut into 2½″×2½″ pieces flat and about ½″ in thickness. Wash thoroughly and dry completely on paper or cloth.
• Heat the ghee and fry sliced onions to a golden brown. Remove and grind with water. In the same ghee fry chopped garlic to a golden brown. Remove and grind with water. Cool the above ghee. Add to it the fried ground onions and garlic. Add all the remaining ingredients, except ghee for basting. Mix well. Add fish pieces and mix well.
• Take a skewer (*seekh*) about 18″ long. Pass the skewer through the centre of each piece of the fish. Pack the pieces closely, levelling the *masala* in between the pieces. With a string tie the pieces, first from one end of the skewer to the other end and then around the pieces, to keep them firm while cooking.
• Light a layer of charcoals and let them burn until white ash appears on the surface. Rest the skewer on some platform, at both ends of the fire, so that the fish pieces remain 6″ above the fire. Keep on rotating the skewer to cook evenly. When the fish pieces become light brown, baste them with the ghee, a little at a time, till all the ghee finishes. Reduce the heat and keep on rotating till the fish pieces become well-browned.
• Remove the string. Gently take out the fish pieces, few at a time, into a pan. Give *dhungar*, method No. 3.
• Some of the ghee and *masala* will drop on the coals and burn. The smoke rising from this gives a typical smoky flavour.

* Picture on page 106.

Machchhi ke Kabab

Preparation time: 30 minutes • Cooking time: 1 hour • To serve: 6 persons.

½ kg. Fish pieces
3 gms. Mustard ground with water
9 gms. Salt
9 gms. Red chillies powdered
12 gms. Ginger scraped and ground

12 gms. Garlic ground
3 gms. Cumin seeds powdered
20 Pepper corns powdered
5 Cloves powdered
3 gms. Fresh mint leaves ground

1 Large egg
60 gms. Onions thinly and evenly sliced
115 gms. Mustard oil.

- Skin the fish, remove bones and cut into pieces. Put the fish in a colander or sieve. Place the colander on an utensil containing so much water that it should not come upto the colander. Cover and steam cook till tender. Remove and mash it thoroughly with hand.
- Add mustard, salt, red chillies, ginger, garlic, cumin seeds, pepper corns, cloves, mint leaves and egg to the fish and mix well.
- Heat the mustard oil and fry onions to a golden brown. Remove, grind and add to the fish. Divide into 12 equal parts. Flatten, wetting hands with a little water to give the kababs a smooth and even shape.
- In the same oil fry the kababs, a few at a time, on low heat till well-browned.

Note: Grind mustard with water and mix in salt. Keep it for 12 hours before cooking.

Machchhi Kabab Sailana

This easy simple quick recipe originates from Sailana. It makes an excellent snack with drinks.

Preparation time: 1 hour • Cooking time: 30 minutes • To serve: 6 persons.

½ kg. Fish pieces
175 gms. Onions finely chopped
25 gms. Ginger scraped and finely chopped
25 gms. Green chillies finely chopped with seeds

12 gms. Fresh coriander leaves finely chopped
45 mls. (1½ ozs.) Vinegar
12 gms. Salt

2 Eggs
Bread crumbs
115 gms. Ghee for frying fish.

• Skin the fish, remove bones and cut into 3"×2" pieces flat and about 1" in thickness. Wash thoroughly and dry completely on paper or cloth.

• Soak chopped onions in vinegar for an hour, so that vinegar gets absorbed in the onions. In the onions add ginger, green chillies, coriander leaves and salt, and mix thoroughly.

• Beat eggs lightly in a separate pan and keep aside. Apply the onion mixture thinly and evenly on both sides of the fish pieces. One by one, dip into eggs and coat well with bread crumbs. Shake off surplus crumbs. Press lightly from all sides to make the coating firm and also to give even shape to the kababs. Keep for half an hour to let the egg coating dry.

• In a frying pan heat the ghee and fry the kababs, 3 to 4 at a time on a moderate heat to a golden brown.

Machchhi ka Khagina*

Preparation time: 1 hour • Cooking time: 30 minutes • To serve: 4 – 6 persons.

- ½ kg. Fish minced
- 60 gms. Ghee
- 60 gms. Onions finely chopped
- 6 gms. Garlic finely chopped
- 12 gms. Green chillies with seeds finely chopped
- 60 mls. (2 ozs.) Tomato ketchup
- 12 gms. Salt
- 1½ gms. Pepper corns powdered
- A good pinch of Mace powdered
- 25 gms. Bread crumbs
- 90 mls. (3 ozs.) milk
- 2 Large eggs beaten lightly Bread crumbs for top dressing.

- Skin the fish, remove bones and cut into pieces. Wash thoroughly and dry completely on paper or cloth. Mince the fish finely.
- Heat the ghee and add onions, garlic and green chillies. Cook on low heat till tender. Add tomato ketchup and cook for another 10 minutes. Cool.
- Add all the remaining ingredients. Add fish and mix thoroughly.
- Grease lightly a 6″ round baking pan and put fish in it spreading and pressing lightly to give even shape. Sprinkle bread crumbs on top.
- In a pre-heated oven bake it on medium heat for half an hour or until it becomes firm and golden brown. Halfway during baking prick the fish with a fork to evaporate moisture. Cool a bit. Loosen the sides of the *khagina* with a knife blade, before turning it out in a serving plate. Cut into pieces.
- Can be served hot as well as cold. Ideal for breakfast or as a snack.

* Picture on page 106.

Khargosh ka Keema

Preparation time: 1 hour ● Cooking time: 1½ hours ● To serve: 6 – 8 persons.

½ kg. Hare boiled and boned
225 gms. Ghee
15 gms. Salt
15 gms. Red chillies powdered

15 gms. Coriander seeds powdered
3 gms. Turmeric
30 gms. Ginger scraped and finely chopped

60 gms. Garlic finely chopped
60 gms. Fresh raw mangoes finely chopped *or*
115 gms. Curd.

● Boil the hare till it is well-cooked and water dries up. In case a little water remains that should be used in *bhunao*. Grind the meat very finely. If necessary, a little water may be added in the process. Mix in the meat all the ingredients except ghee.

● Heat the ghee, add the meat and cook on low fire stirring it regularly. *Bhunao* till meat becomes well-browned and water dries up completely.

● Instead of hare, rabbit may be cooked as above.

Khargosh Khatta

Preparation time: 1 hour • Cooking time: 1½ hours • To serve: 4 – 6 persons.

½ kg. Hare cut into about 2½"×2½" pieces
115 gms. Ghee
2 2" Cinnamon sticks whole
4 Bay leaves whole

12 gms. Salt
3 gms. Pepper corns whole
6 gms. Red chillies whole
6 gms. Coriander seeds coarsely ground

115 gms. Onions thinly and evenly sliced
25 gms. Garlic whole
12 gms. Ginger scraped and shredded
250 gms. Curd well beaten.

• Heat the ghee and add cinnamon and bay leaves. Add the meat along with salt, pepper corns, red chillies, and coriander seeds. Add only as much water that it should dry up when meat is tender.

• When tender, add all the remaining ingredients and simmer on low fire till the gravy becomes thick and ghee floats on top of it.

• Rabbit may also be cooked as above.

Khargosh ka Keema Nizami

I am grateful to Late Hakim Nizamuddin Khan Sahib of Ajmer for giving me this fine recipe.

Preparation time: 2 hours ● Cooking time: 1 hour ● To serve: 6 – 8 persons.

½ kg. Finely minced meat of hare (*Keema*)

115 gms. Curd

15 gms. Salt

12 gms. Red chillies powdered

18 gms. Kachri ground with water

12 gms. Parched grams powdered

15 gms. Raw papaya peeled and ground with water

12 gms. Ginger scraped and ground

3 gms. *Garam masala* powder

175 gms. Ghee

115 gms. Onions thinly and evenly sliced

15 gms. Green chillies finely chopped with seeds

1½ gms. Fresh mint leaves finely chopped

3 gms. Fresh coriander leaves finely chopped.

● Mix thoroughly curd, salt, red chillies, kachri, parched grams, papaya, ginger and *garam masala* powder into the meat and marinade for an hour.

● Heat the ghee and fry sliced onions to a golden brown. Add marinaded meat and simmer on low heat stirring regularly. No water to be added. When meat becomes brown, add green chillies, mint leaves and coriander leaves. Put on hot ashes with live charcoals on top of the lid till liquids dry up completely.

● Give *dhungar*, method No. 2.

● For preserving it, cool it completely and keep in some glass or enamelled jar. Make it warm whenever to be eaten. It can be kept for at least 15 days in cold weather and about a week in summer. Ideal for camp life.

● Instead of hare, rabbit or game meat can be cooked as above.

Khargosh ki Mokal

Preparation time: 1 hour ● Cooking time: 2 hours ● To serve: 6 – 8 persons.

½ kg. Hare boiled and boned
175 gms. Ghee
115 gms. Onions thinly and evenly sliced
115 gms. Curd
12 gms. Salt
12 gms. Red chillies powdered

12 gms. Kachri powdered
6 gms. Coriander seeds powdered
3 gms. Turmeric
3 gms. Cumin seeds
25 gms. Garlic ground
12 gms. Ginger scraped and ground

25 gms. Almonds blanched and ground with water
1½ gms. Cardamom seeds ground dry
1½ gms. *Garam masala* powder.

● Cut the hare into large pieces and boil well in so much water that it should dry up when hare is tender. Remove bones and all the white membranes from the surface of the meat. Shred the meat pieces into thin long fibres.

● Heat the ghee and fry sliced onions to a golden brown. Add all the ingredients, except cardamoms and *garam masala* powder, and *bhunao* till well-browned and ghee separates from the *masala*.

● Then add the shredded meat and stir. Add one cup of water and simmer it on low fire till water dries up. Add cardamom and *garam masala* powder.

● Rabbit may be cooked as above.

Khargosh ki Mokal (Dry)*

Preparation time: 30 minutes • Cooking time: 2 hours • To serve: 6 – 8 persons.

½ kg. Hare boiled and boned	12 gms. Red chillies powdered	1½ gms. Cardamom seeds powdered dry
115 gms. Ghee	3 gms. Cumin seeds powdered	A pinch of Saffron diluted in warm water.
12 gms. Salt		

• Cut the hare in large pieces and boil well in only as much water that it should dry up when meat is cooked. Remove bones and all the white membranes from the surface of the meat. Shred the meat pieces into thin long fibres.

• Heat the ghee and fry the shredded meat on low heat. When crisp, add all the ingredients, mix well and remove from the fire.

• Rabbit may be cooked as above.

* Picture on page 105.

Sabat Khargosh (Whole)*

Preparation time: 30 minutes ● Cooking time: 2 hours ● To serve: 10 – 12 persons.

1 Hare whole about 1½ kg. in weight	6 2″ Cinnamon sticks whole	9 gms. Turmeric
350 gms. Ghee	6 Bay leaves whole	9 gms. Cumin seeds
175 gms. Onions thinly and evenly sliced	175 gms. Curd	175 gms. Onions ground
6 Black cardamoms whole	36 gms. Salt	75 gms. Garlic ground
20 Pepper corns whole	36 gms. Red chillies powdered	36 gms. Ginger scraped and ground
10 Cloves whole	36 gms. Coriander seeds powdered	9 gms. *Garam masala* powder.

● Wash and clean the hare. Take out the eyes, and cut off the fore and hind legs at the first joint. Bring the legs close to the body and tie them with string. Prick all over with a fork.

● Heat the ghee and fry the sliced onions to a golden brown, remove, grind dry and keep aside.

● In the same ghee add black cardamoms, pepper corns, cloves, cinnamon and bay leaves, and brown them lightly. Add all the remaining ingredients, except *garam masala* powder, and *bhunao* till well-browned and ghee separates from the *masala*. Add hare and fried ground onions, and so much water that it should dry up when meat is tender.

● Cover and cook, turning the sides of the hare and stirring the *masala* occasionally. When tender and very little water remains, add *garam masala* powder. Reduce heat to the minimum and put live charcoals on top of the lid. Simmer till water dries up and only ghee remains.

● Alternatively, after browning the *masala* put it in a pressure cooker along with the hare, and add 2 cups of water. Cook at 15 lbs. pressure for 20 minutes. Remove from fire and allow the pressure to drop by itself. If some water remains, dry it up cooking on low heat uncovered. Then add *garam masala* powder.

● With the above recipe, rabbit, whole leg or neck of other animals can also be cooked.

Top: Sabat Khargosh (Whole)
Mid-left: Khargosh ka Keema Nizami
Mid-right: Soovar ki Santh
Bottom: Khargosh ki Mokal (Dry)

* *Picture on facing page.*

Khargosh ki Kachar

Preparation time: 1 hour ● Cooking time: 1½ hours ● To serve: 6 – 8 persons.

½ kg. Hare cut and boned
60 gms. Ghee
115 gms. Curd
18 gms. Salt
18 gms. Red chillies powdered

18 gms. Coriander seeds powdered
18 gms. Kachri powdered
3 gms. Turmeric
3 gms. Cumin seeds
115 gms. Onions ground

25 gms. Garlic ground
60 gms. Ghee for *baghar*
6 gms. Ani seeds whole for *baghar*.

● Cut the meat into large pieces and wash thoroughly. Remove bones completely. Then cut the meat into ½″ pieces.

● Put the meat in the pan and add curd, salt, red chillies, coriander seeds, kachri, turmeric, cumin seeds, onion and garlic. Mash it with hand. Gradually add water and keep on mashing for about 15 minutes, adding in all, about 6 pints (12 cups) of water. In between, keep on removing all the white membranes from the mixture. Add ghee.

● Put on fire and keep on stirring till it starts boiling. Cover and cook. Add more water if necessary. When cooked and gravy becomes thick, remove from fire.

● In a separate pan heat the ghee for *baghar*. Add ani seeds and when they turn dark brown, put the ghee along with ani seeds into the meat and stir. Alternative *baghar* of cumin seeds or chopped garlic may be given.

Notes: 1. Can also be made of sand grouse.
2. To be served preferably with *bajra* or *makai roti*.

Top: Machchhi ka Soola
Middle: Machchhi ka Khagina
Bottom: Mahi Kabab Kalia

Soovar ki Santh*

Preparation time: 1 hour • Cooking time: 1½ hours • To serve: 6 – 8 persons.

½ kg. Fresh pig skin with fat cut into 2″×2″ pieces
60 gms. Ghee
115 gms. Onions thinly and evenly sliced
15 gms. Salt
15 gms. Red chillies powdered
6 gms. Coriander seeds powdered
3 gms. Cumin seeds whole
3 gms. Turmeric
12 gms. Ginger scraped and ground
25 gms. Garlic ground
1½ gms. *Garam masala* powder
2 tbsp. Fresh coriander leaves chopped.

• Remove hair and deposits from the skin by dipping it in boiling water frequently and scrubbing with a knife. Prick the pieces well with a fork.
• Boil them in pressure cooker with 6 cups of water at 15 lbs. pressure for 20 minutes. Remove pig skin and keep aside. Discard the water.
• In a separate pan heat the ghee and fry sliced onions to a golden brown. Remove, grind and keep aside.
• In the same ghee add all the ingredients, except *garam masala* powder and coriander leaves. *Bhunao* till well-browned. Add pig skin, fried ground onions and 2 cups of water. Cook on low fire, stirring regularly till the water dries up completely. Add *garam masala* powder and chopped coriander leaves.

Note: This can be obtained from pork shop.

* Picture on page 105.

Biryani Rashmi

Preparation time: 1 hour ● Cooking time: 2 hours ● To serve: 8 – 10 persons.

1 kg. Mutton pieces	25 gms. Coriander seeds powdered	A good pinch of Saffron diluted in warm water
250 gms. Ghee	12 gms. Panjabi badi powdered	$\frac{1}{2}$ kg. Basmati rice
350 gms. Curd		60 gms. Salt for rice
25 gms. Salt	$1\frac{1}{2}$ gms. Cumin seeds powdered	30 mls. (1 oz.) Kewada water
6 gms. Red chillies powdered	$1\frac{1}{2}$ gms. Black cumin seeds powdered	360 mls. (12 ozs.) Milk.
25 gms. Ginger scraped and ground	$1\frac{1}{2}$ gms. Cloves powdered	
2 grains of Asafoetida (*Hing*) of the size of pepper corn diluted in water	$1\frac{1}{2}$ gms. Black cardamoms powdered	

● Heat the ghee. Add meat along with curd, salt, red chillies, ginger and asafoetida. When liquids dry up, lightly brown the meat. Add only as much water that it should dry up when meat is tender. When tender and very little water remains, add coriander seeds, Panjabi badi, cumin seeds, black cumin seeds, cloves, black cardamoms and saffron, and stir. Simmer on low heat till water dries up completely and only ghee remains.

● Wash and soak the rice in deep water for an hour. Boil the rice in plenty of water adding salt. When just cooked, drain in a sieve or colander removing water completely. Spread the rice in a wide dish and cool a bit.

● Divide the cooked rice in four parts. Grease the bottom and sides of a heavy-bottomed pan with a little ghee. Spread one part of rice evenly. Add kewada water to the milk and sprinkle it over the rice. Then spread half of the meat over the rice. Cover it with two more parts of rice and spread the remaining meat over this. Now spread the remaining part of the rice. Cover the pan and put it on medium fire to form steam. As soon as steam rises, put on *dum* for half an hour.

Malai ki Biryani*

As the name suggests this Biryani is rich and delicious. I would not recommend it to weight watchers.

Preparation time: 1 hour ● Cooking time: 2 hours ● To serve: 8 – 10 persons.

Ingredients for Mutton

1 kg. Lean mutton from saddle and leg, cut into pasandas
115 gms. Ghee
250 gms. Curd
25 gms. Salt
18 gms. Red chillies powdered
12 gms. Coriander seeds powdered

6 gms. Cumin seeds whole
6 gms. *Garam masala* powder
1½ gms. Cardamom seeds powdered
25 gms. Ginger scraped and ground
18 gms. Dry figs ground with water

18 gms. Raisins ground with water
30 gms. Khoa
A good pinch of Asafoetida diluted in water
30 mls. (1 oz.) Vinegar

Ingredients for Rice

½ kg. Basmati rice

36 gms. Salt

6 gms. Alum powdered

Ingredients for Layers

120 mls. (4 ozs.) Milk
60 gms. Ghee for rice

½ kg. *Rabree*(Thick evaporated milk)

15 mls. (½ oz.) Kewada water
6 Silver varaks.

● Prepare meat pasandas as described in Recipe No. 8. Cook meat along with ghee, curd, salt, red chillies, coriander seeds, cumin seeds, *garam masala* powder, cardamoms, ginger, dry figs, raisins, khoa, asafoetida, and vinegar on a low heat. No water to be added. When cooked, dry the liquids completely. Keep aside.

● Wash and soak rice in deep water for half an hour. Boil rice in plenty of water along with salt and alum. When three-fourths cooked, drain in a sieve or colander removing water completely. Spread rice in wide dish and cool a bit.

● Grease a heavy-bottomed pan with a little ghee, bottom and sides. Spread one-third rice evenly. Put milk. Over the rice spread half of the meat. Put second layer of rice and repeat as above. After final layer of rice put a wet cloth over the rice covering them completely. Cover the pan and put on medium fire to form steam. As soon as steam rises, sprinkle ghee. Put on *dum* for half an hour. Serve rice in a plate and spread *rabree* evenly

* Picture on page 123.

over the rice covering it completely. Sprinkle kewada water. Put on silver varak.

• *Rabree* can be obtained from any sweetmeat shop. Place order 12 hours before cooking time, to prepare thick *rabree* without sugar, colour or flavourings. Keep it in a warm place. Not to be put in refrigerator.

84

Biryani Khaibari

Our foods have many foreign influences. Dishes from neighbouring countries have reached to our kitchens with the various invasions. This biryani belongs to the Pathans and has found its way to us through the Khaiber Pass.

Preparation time: 2½ hours • Cooking time: 2 hours • To serve: 8 – 10 persons.

1 kg. Lean mutton from saddle and leg cut into pasandas	40 Pepper corns powdered	120 gms. Ghee for *baghar*
25 gms. Salt	3 gms. Black cumin seeds powdered	20 Cloves whole
25 gms. Ginger scraped and ground	2 2″ Cinnamon sticks powdered	½ kg. Basmati rice
120 gms. Onions ground	A good pinch of Saffron diluted in warm water	12 gms. Salt for rice
25 gms. Coriander seeds powdered	½ kg. Curd fresh and thick	½ kg. Curd fresh and thick for rice
2 Black cardamoms powdered	120 mls. (4 ozs.) Water	120 gms. Ghee for rice.

• Prepare meat pasandas as described in Recipe No. 8. Cut the pasandas into 2″×2″ size pieces. Add salt, ginger and onions to the meat. Mix well and marinade for two hours. Mix thoroughly coriander seeds, black cardamoms, pepper corns, black cumin seeds, cinnamon, saffron, curd and water, and add to the meat.

• Put the meat into a heavy-bottomed pan, spreading evenly. In a separate pan heat the ghee for *baghar* and add cloves. When they turn dark brown pour the ghee, with cloves on to the meat. Do not stir.

• Dilute salt in one cup of water and add to the rice. Rub them with hands thoroughly. Wash them twice in fresh water and drain. Add curd to the rice and mix well. Spread the rice over the meat evenly. Cover the pan and put on medium fire to form steam. As soon as steam rises put on *dum* till the curd dries up completely. Add ghee to the rice and keep on *dum* for another 15 minutes.

Note: The rice is cooked in curd, no water is added.

Mewe ki Biryani

Preparation time: 1 hour ● Cooking time: 2 hours ● To serve: 8 – 10 persons.

½ kg. Basmati rice
36 gms. Salt for rice
½ kg. Minced lean mutton from leg or shoulder (*Keema*)
120 gms. Ghee
120 gms. Onions thinly and evenly sliced
12 gms. Salt for mutton
6 gms. Red chillies powdered
12 gms. Coriander seeds powdered

12 gms. Garlic ground
12 gms. Ginger ground
120 gms. Curd
3 gms. *Garam masala* powder
30 gms. Almonds blanched and shredded
30 gms. Pistachios blanched and shredded
or
30 gms. Charoli blanched whole

60 gms. Raisins cut into halves
60 gms. Coconut grated and roasted dry
60 gms. Khoa roasted dry
60 mls. (2 ozs.) Lime juice
240 mls. (8 ozs.) Milk
30 mls. (1 oz.) Kewada water.

● Wash and soak the rice in water for an hour. Boil the rice in plenty of water adding salt. When just cooked, drain in a sieve or colander removing water completely. Spread the rice in a wide dish and cool a bit.

● Heat the ghee and fry sliced onions to a golden brown. Add minced meat along with salt, red chillies, coriander seeds, garlic, ginger and curd. *Bhunao* till meat is well-browned. Add water and cook. When tender, dry the water completely. Add *garam masala* powder.

● In a separate pan mix almonds, pistachios, raisins, coconut, khoa and lime juice, and keep aside.

● Grease a heavy-bottomed pan with a little ghee, bottom and sides. Put one-fifth of the rice spreading evenly. Add kewada water to the milk and sprinkle over the rice. Over the rice spread half of the meat. Then put second layer of rice. Over the rice spread half of the dry fruits mixture. Repeat as above. After final layer of rice put a wet cloth covering the rice completely.

● Cover the pan and put on medium fire to form steam. As soon as steam rises put on *dum* for half an hour.

Machchhi ki Biryani

Preparation time: 1 hour • Cooking time: 2 hours • To serve: 8 – 10 persons.

1 kg. Fish boned and cut into pieces. Any firm white fish	25 gms. Ginger scraped and ground	1½ gms. Pepper corns powdered
250 gms. Ghee	6 gms. Cumin seeds powdered	30 mls. (1 oz.) Kewada water
250 gms. Onions thinly and evenly sliced	3 gms. Cinnamon powdered	A pinch of Saffron diluted in warm water
250 gms. Curd	3 gms. Ani seeds powdered	½ kg. Basmati rice
18 gms. Salt		30 gms. Salt in boiling rice
25 gms. Coriander seeds powdered	3 gms. Black cardamoms powdered	120 mls. (4 ozs.) Milk.
	1½ gms. Cloves powdered	

- Skin the fish, remove bones and cut into pieces. Wash thoroughly and dry completely on paper or cloth.
- Heat the ghee and fry sliced onions to a golden brown. Remove, grind and keep aside.
- In the same ghee add curd, salt, coriander seeds, ginger, cumin seeds, cinnamon, ani seeds, black cardamoms, cloves and pepper corns,and stir. When it starts boiling,add fish and fried ground onions. No water to be added. Cook uncovered on medium fire stirring occasionally and gently not to break the pieces. Cook till fish is tender and only ghee remains. Add kewada water and saffron.
- Wash and soak the rice in deep water for an hour. Boil the rice in plenty of water adding salt. When just cooked, drain in a sieve or colander removing water completely. Spread rice in a wide dish and cool a bit.
- Grease a heavy-bottomed pan with a little ghee, bottom and sides. Put one-third of rice spreading evenly. Sprinkle milk over the rice.
- Put half of the fish spreading evenly on rice. Over it spread one-third of rice and then remaining half of the fish. Now spread the remaining one-third of rice.
- Put a wet cloth over the rice covering it completely. Cover and put on medium heat for 15 minutes. When steam is formed put on *dum* for half an hour.

Pulao Noor Mahal

Preparation time: 1 hour • Cooking time: 2 hours • To serve: 8 – 10 persons.

Ingredients for *Yakhni*

1 kg. Mutton pieces	30 gms. Ginger scraped and ground	5 2" Cinnamon sticks powdered
60 gms. Onions ground		
60 gms. Garlic ground	30 gms. Coriander seeds powdered	18 gms. Salt for *yakhni*
		240 mls. (8 ozs.) Milk

Ingredients for Mutton

115 gms. Ghee for mutton	30 gms. Almonds blanched and thinly sliced	9 gms. Cardamoms powdered
60 gms. Onions thinly and evenly sliced		
30 gms. Almonds blanched and ground with water	30 gms. Ginger scraped and thinly sliced	15 mls. (½ oz.) Kewada water
	115 gms. *Malai*	12 gms. Salt

Ingredients for Rice

240 mls. (8 ozs.) Milk for rice	10 Cardamoms whole	15 mls. (½ oz.) Kewada water
25 gms. Ghee for *baghar*	½ kg. Basmati rice	
10 Cloves whole	6 gms. Alum powder	115 gms. Ghee for rice.

• Boil meat in plenty of water for 5 minutes. Discard the water and wash the meat in fresh water. Boil the meat again in fresh water along with onions, garlic, ginger, coriander seeds, cinnamon, salt and milk. When meat is tender remove from the liquid and keep aside. Strain the liquid through a muslin. The quantity of the liquid should be three-fourths cup. Cook extra if more. Add water if less. This is known as *yakhni*.

• Heat the ghee and fry sliced onions to a golden brown. Remove and keep aside. In the same ghee add boiled meat along with ground almonds, sliced almonds, ginger, *malai*, cardamoms, kewada water and salt, and stir. Simmer on low fire till the liquid dries up completely.

• In a separate pan boil milk till it reduces to half. Keep aside.

• In a separate pan heat the ghee for *baghar* and add cloves and cardamoms. When they turn dark brown, add plenty of water to cook the rice. When it starts boiling, add rice and alum and stir. When the rice is half-cooked, drain in a sieve or colander removing water completely.

• Spread rice over the meat. Mix *yakhni*, milk and kewada water, and pour over the rice. Cover the pan and put on medium heat to form steam. As soon as steam rises add ghee and fried onions. Then put on *dum* for half an hour.

88

Soola Pulao

Preparation time: 1 hour • Cooking time: 2 hours • To serve: 8 – 10 persons.

½ kg. Mutton pieces
3 gms. Salt for mutton
60 gms. Onion pieces
12 gms. Garlic chopped
6 gms. Ginger chopped
6 gms. Coriander seeds whole

½ kg. Basmati rice
60 gms. Ghee
25 gms. Salt for rice
1 kg. Cooked soola (Recipe No. 27) or Machchhi ka Soola (Recipe No. 70)

240 mls. (8 ozs.) Milk
15 mls. (½ oz.) Rose water
60 gms. Ghee.

• Boil meat in plenty of water, along with salt, for 5 minutes. Discard water and wash the meat twice in fresh water. Boil the meat again in fresh water along with onions, garlic, ginger and coriander seeds. When meat is tender, strain the liquid through a muslin squeezing meat well to extract maximum flavour. Discard the meat. The liquid should be 6 cups. If less add water, if more dry it by cooking. You have prepared the *yakhni*.

• In a pan put *yakhni*. When it starts boiling, add rice, ghee and salt, and stir. Cover and cook on medium heat. When three-fourths cooked, put on hot ashes and some live charcoals on top of the lid and simmer till the liquid dries up.

• Grease a heavy-bottomed pan with a little ghee, bottom and sides. Put one-third of rice spreading evenly. Add rose water to the milk and sprinkle over the rice. Spread half of the soola evenly over the rice. Spread one-third of rice and then the remaining half of the soola. Spread remaining one-third of the rice. Cover the pan and put on medium fire to form steam. As soon as steam rises, sprinkle ghee over the rice. Put on *dum* for half an hour.

Aam ka Pulao

Like the other mango dishes this excellent pulao impacts a sweet and sour taste so welcome in the hot season.

Preparation time: 1 hour • Cooking time: 2 hours • To serve: 8 – 10 persons.

½ kg. Mutton pieces
25 gms. Salt
12 gms. Red chillies powdered
12 gms. Coriander seeds powdered
115 gms. Onions ground
12 gms. Ginger scraped and ground
60 gms. Ghee for *baghar*
5 Cloves whole
350 gms. Raw mangoes peeled, shelled and cut into 2" slices

350 gms. Sugar
250 gms. Finely minced lean mutton from leg *or* shoulder (*Keema*)
6 gms. Salt
6 gms. Red chillies powdered
12 gms. Split grams (*Chana dal*)
60 gms. Khoa
115 gms. Ghee for frying kababs

60 gms. Onions thinly and evenly sliced
25 gms. Almonds blanched and sliced
25 gms. Charoli blanched whole
25 gms. Raisins cut into halves
½ kg. Basmati rice
3 gms. *Garam masala* powder.

• Prepare *yakhni* as follows: Boil meat in water along with salt, red chillies, coriander seeds, onions, and ginger. When meat is tender, remove from the liquid and keep aside. Add to the liquid one-third of the sliced mangoes and cook till tender. Strain the liquid through a muslin, squeezing mangoes well to extract maximum flavour. The quantity of the liquid should be 6 cups. If less add water, if more dry it by cooking. Heat the ghee for *baghar* and add cloves. When they turn dark brown, put the ghee along with cloves, into the liquid.

• In a separate pan put sugar and 3 cups of water. Cook, stirring till syrup gets one-thread consistency. Keep aside.

• In a separate pan boil water. Add remaining two-thirds sliced mangoes, stir and at once drain off the water. Add mango slices to sugar syrup and stir. Cook on low fire till just tender. Remove mango slices from the syrup and keep aside. Add the syrup to the *yakhni* and stir.

• In a separate pan cook minced meat along with salt, red chillies and split grams. When tender, dry the liquid completely. Grind the meat

finely with khoa. Divide
into 20 equal parts. Flatten, wetting hands with a
little water to give the kababs a smooth and even shape.
Heat the ghee in a frying pan. Fry the kababs, a few at a time, to
a golden brown. Remove and keep aside.

- In the same ghee fry sliced onions to a golden brown. Remove and keep aside. In the same ghee fry almonds and raisins separately and keep aside.
- In a separate pan cook rice in plenty of water. When half-cooked, drain in a sieve or colander removing water completely.
- In a heavy-bottomed pan spread the meat evenly. Sprinkle *garam masala* powder over the meat. Spread half of the rice over the meat. Put kababs over the rice. Spread remaining half of the rice. Sprinkle *yakhni*.
- Cover and cook on low fire for 15 minutes. Then spread over the rice mango slices, almonds, raisins and fried onions evenly in that order. Sprinkle ghee in which kababs were fried, over the rice.
- Put on *dum* for half an hour.
- Before serving toss the rice gently, without breaking them.

Khichdi Shahjehani

Preparation time: 1 hour • Cooking time: 2 hours • To serve: 8 – 10 persons.

Ingredients for Mutton

750 gms. Minced lean mutton from leg *or* shoulder (*Keema*)
175 gms. Ghee for mutton
18 gms. Salt
9 gms. Red chillies powdered
30 gms. Onions ground

18 gms. Ginger scraped and ground
12 gms. Garlic ground
175 gms. Curd
18 gms. Coriander seeds powdered and roasted dry

3 gms. Black cumin seeds powdered
1½ gms. Cardamom seeds powdered
6 gms. *Garam masala* powder
3 gms. Fresh mint leaves chopped

Ingredients for Rice

175 gms. Ghee for rice
60 gms. Onions thinly and evenly sliced
30 gms. Onions ground for rice

18 gms. Ginger scraped and ground for rice
12 gms. Garlic ground for rice
½ kg. Basmati rice

250 gms. Split green beans (*Moong dal*) skinless
18 gms. Salt for rice
180 mls. (6 ozs.) Milk.

• In a heavy-bottomed pan heat the ghee and add minced meat along with salt, red chillies, onions, ginger, garlic and curd. *Bhunao* it till well-browned. Add water, cover and cook. When tender and very little water remains, add coriander seeds, black cumin seeds, cardamoms, *garam masala* powder and mint leaves. Put on *dum* till water dries up completely.
• In a separate pan heat ghee and fry sliced onions to a golden brown. Remove and keep aside. In the same ghee add onions, ginger and garlic, and fry till light brown. Add rice and split green beans, and fry till light brown, stirring constantly to avoid sticking to the bottom of the pan. Add water and salt. Cover and cook on medium heat. When half-cooked, put on hot ashes and some live charcoals on the top of the lid. Simmer till three-fourths cooked and liquid dries up. Spread rice over the meat evenly. Add milk. Spread fried onions on top of the rice. Put on *dum* for half an hour. Before serving stir very gently blending meat and rice evenly.

Khichdi Shirazi

Normally the association of Khichdi is with simple easy-to-digest food for sick people, but not so in Persian Cookery. A Khichdi like this one can be as delicious as any pulao.

Preparation time: 1 hour • Cooking time: 2 hours • To serve 8 – 10 persons.

½ kg. Finely Minced lean mutton from leg *or* shoulder (*Keema*)
60 gms. Ghee
12 gms. Salt
36 gms. Coriander seeds whole, ground with water
12 gms. Ginger scraped and ground
½ kg. Basmati rice

30 gms. Salt in boiling rice
175 gms. Curd well beaten
9 gms. Pepper corns powdered
18 gms. Black cumin seeds powdered
1½ gms. Cardamom seeds powdered
1½ gms. Black cardamom seeds powdered
10 Cloves powdered

1½ gms. Saffron diluted in warm water
30 mls. (1 oz.) Kewada water
240 mls. (8 ozs.) Milk
60 gms. Ghee for *baghar*
6 gms. Raisins whole
12 Cardamoms whole
20 Cloves whole.

• Heat the ghee. Add minced meat and stir. Dilute ground coriander seeds and ground ginger in about 4 cups of water. Strain the liquid through a muslin squeezing spices well to extract maximum flavour. Add this liquid to the meat along with salt. Cover and cook on low fire till the meat is tender and the liquids dry up completely. Do not brown the meat.

• Wash and soak the rice in deep water for two hours. Boil the rice in plenty of water adding salt. When just cooked, drain in a sieve or colander removing water completely. Spread the rice in a wide dish and cool a bit.

• Grease a heavy-bottomed pan with a little ghee, bottom and sides. Put minced meat spreading evenly. Over the meat spread curd. Mix well pepper corns, black cumin seeds, cardamoms, black cardamoms, and cloves, and spread over the curd. Mix saffron in kewada water and sprinkle half of it over the curd. Put half of the rice spreading evenly. Sprinkle over the rice remaining half of the saffron. Put the remaining half of the rice spreading evenly. Add milk.

• Put a wet cloth over the rice covering it completely. Cover the pan with a lid and seal the edges of the lid with wheat flour paste.

• Put on *dum* for an hour.

• In a separate pan heat the ghee for *baghar*. Add raisins, cardamoms and cloves. When they turn dark brown, remove from ghee and discard. Add the above ghee to the rice.

• Gently toss the rice in such a way that all ingredients get evenly mixed without smashing the rice.

Lahasun Pulao*

A very unusual dish. In spite of the huge quantity of Garlic the cooked pulao imparts a unique flavour. People not too fond of Garlic begin to love it after trying this once.

Preparation time: 1 hour • Cooking time: 2 hours • To serve: 8 – 10 persons.

Ingredients for *Yakhni*

½ kg. Mutton pieces
12 gms. Salt
6 gms. Coriander seeds

6 gms. Ginger scraped and ground
12 gms. Garlic ground

60 gms. Onions ground
60 gms. Ghee for *baghar*
5 Cloves whole

Ingredients for Mutton

60 gms. Ghee for mutton
60 gms. Onions thinly and evenly sliced
3 gms. Salt
6 gms. Coriander seeds powdered

6 gms. Ginger scraped and ground
20 Pepper corns, powdered
4 2" Cinnamon sticks powdered
1½ gms. Cumin seeds powdered

5 gms. Cloves powdered
5 Cardamoms powdered
A pinch of Saffron diluted in warm water

Ingredients for Rice

10 Cloves whole
10 Cardamoms whole
15 gms. Salt

15 gms. Alum powdered
60 gms. Ghee in boiling rice

½ kg. Basmati rice
250 gms. Garlic whole

Ingredients for Layers

A pinch of Saffron diluted in warm water

180 gms. Ghee for rice.

• Wash and soak the rice in deep water for three hours. Cut each garlic whole into four pieces. Soak in deep water for three hours.

• Prepare *yakhni* as follows: Boil meat in water along with salt, coriander seeds, ginger, garlic and onions. When meat is tender, the quantity of liquid should be reduced to two cups. Cook extra if more, add water if less. Remove meat from the liquid and keep aside.

• Heat the ghee for *baghar* and add cloves. When they turn dark brown put the ghee along with cloves into the liquid. Strain the liquid through a muslin squeezing spices well to extract maximum flavour.

• In a separate heavy-bottomed pan heat the ghee for meat and fry sliced

* *Picture on page 123.*

onions to a golden brown.
Add boiled meat along with salt, coriander seeds,
ginger, pepper corns, cinnamon, cumin seeds, cloves, cardamoms
and saffron, and stir. Simmer on low fire for about 5 minutes.

- In a separate pan boil water along with cloves, cardamoms, salt, alum and ghee. When water starts boiling, add rice and garlic pieces. When the rice is three-fourths cooked, drain in a sieve or colander, along with garlic pieces, removing water completely. Spread in a wide dish and cool a bit.
- Spread rice and garlic over the meat. Add *yakhni,* cover the pan and put on medium fire to form steam. As soon as steam rises, add saffron and ghee and put on *dum* for half an hour.

Shola Pulao*

Preparation time: 1 hour • Cooking time: 2 hours • To serve: 8 – 10 persons.

60 gms. Ghee	30 gms. Split grams (*Chana dal*)	120 gms. Green peas fresh and shelled
120 gms. Onions thinly and evenly sliced	120 gms. Spinach chopped	30 gms. Salt
½ kg. Mutton pieces	120 gms. Turnips peeled and cut into ½" pieces	1½ gms. Black cumin seeds whole
9 gms. Coriander seeds powdered	120 gms. Carrots peeled and cut into ½" pieces	60 Pepper corns powdered
18 gms. Ginger scraped and ground	120 gms. Beetroots peeled and cut into ½" pieces	10 Cloves powdered
30 gms. Split green beans (*Moong dal*) skinless	60 gms. Ghee for *baghar*	4 2" Cinnamon sticks powdered
30 gms. Red lentils (*Masur dal*)	5 Cloves whole	20 Cardamoms powdered
	½ kg. Basmati rice	120 mls. (4 ozs.) Milk
		5 Cloves whole
		120 gms. Ghee for rice.

• Prepare *yakhni* as follows: Heat the ghee and fry sliced onions to a golden brown. Add meat along with coriander seeds, ginger, split green beans, red lentils, split grams and spinach, and enough water to cook the meat. Stir and cook. When meat is half-cooked, add turnips, carrots and beetroots. When meat is tender, remove it from the liquid and keep aside. Remove turnips, carrots and beetroots and keep aside. Strain the liquid through a muslin, squeezing spices well to extract maximum flavour. The liquid should be 1 litre.

• Heat the ghee for *baghar* and add cloves. When they turn dark brown, put the ghee along with cloves into the strained liquid (*yakhni*) and stir. Add rice to it along with green peas and salt and stir. Cover and cook on medium heat. When three-fourths cooked, put on hot ashes and some live charcoal on top of the lid and simmer till liquid dries up.

• In a separate pan sprinkle black cumin seeds and spread the meat pieces evenly. Sprinkle pepper corns, cloves, cinnamon and cardamom over the meat. Do not stir. Spread rice, with peas, evenly over the meat. Add milk. Spread over the rice turnips, carrots and beetroots. Cover the pan and put on medium fire to form steam. As soon as steam rises, put on *dum* for half an hour.

• Heat the ghee and add cloves, when they turn dark brown sprinkle ghee over the rice.

• Before serving toss the rice gently without breaking them, blending meat and vegetable evenly.

Top: Lahasun Pulao
Middle: Malai ki Biryani
Bottom: Shola Pulao

* *Picture on facing page.*

Makki ka Soyta*

Preparation time: 1 hour ● Cooking time: 2 hours ● To serve: 8 – 10 persons.

½ kg. Mutton pieces
½ kg. Fresh corn kernels grated
175 gms. Ghee
6 Cloves whole
4 Black cardamoms whole
2 2″ Cinnamon sticks whole
2 Bay leaves whole
115 gms. Curd

25 gms. Salt
6 gms. Red chillies powdered
12 gms. Coriander seeds powdered
3 gms. Turmeric
3 gms. Cumin seeds whole
60 gms. Onions ground
25 gms. Garlic ground

12 gms. Green chillies chopped finely with seeds
15 gms. Sugar
240 mls. (8 ozs.) Milk
60 gms. Gram flour diluted in water
15 mls. (½ oz.) Lime juice
1 tbsp. Fresh coriander leaves chopped.

● Take fresh and tender corn. Grate the kernels, but not finely. Keep aside.

● Heat the ghee. Add cloves, black cardamoms, cinnamon and bay leaves. After a while add meat along with curd, salt, red chillies, coriander seeds, turmeric, cumin seeds, onions and garlic. *Bhunao* the meat till it is well-browned.

● Add enough water to cook the meat. When meat is almost tender, add grated corn kernels and green chillies, sugar, milk and gram flour, and stir well. Add enough water to cook the kernels. Cook on medium heat, stirring all the time to avoid kernels sticking to the bottom of the pan. The kernels are cooked when they do not stick any more to the bottom of the pan, and ghee films on the surface.

● Add lime juice and coriander leaves and stir well.

Top: Mutanjan Pulao
Middle: Sewian ki Biryani
Bottom: Makki ka Soyta

Picture on facing page.

Mutanjan Pulao*

One of the oldest pulaos and the grandest. Sweet, sour and chillies all blend to give it an unusual and excellent taste.

Preparation time: 1½ hours ● Cooking time: 2½ hours ● To serve: 8 – 10 persons.

Ingredients for *Yakhni*

½ kg. Mutton pieces
2 Black cardamoms coarsely powdered
20 Pepper corns coarsely powdered
5 Cloves coarsely powdered

1 1" Cinnamon stick coarsely powdered
1½ gms. Ani seeds coarsely powdered
1½ gms. Cumin seeds coarsely powdered
1½ gms. Mace coarsely powdered

6 gms. Coriander seeds coarsely powdered
2 Bay leaves
30 gms. Onions ground
6 gms. Garlic ground
6 gms. Ginger ground

Ingredients for Mutton

60 gms. Ghee
12 gms. Salt
12 gms. Red chillies powdered

115 gms. Curd
18 gms. Ginger scraped and ground
12 gms. Coriander seeds powdered

12 gms. Panjabi badi powdered
6 gms. *Garam masala* powder

Ingredients for Rice

½ kg. Basmati rice

25 gms. Salt in rice

60 gms. Ghee in rice

Ingredients for Kababs

250 gms. Minced lean mutton from leg *or* shoulder (*Keema*)

12 gms. Split grams (*Chana dal*)
6 gms. Salt
6 gms. Red chillies powdered

60 gms. Khoa
Ghee for frying kababs
6 Silver varaks

Ingredients for Layers

250 gms. Sugar powdered
60 mls. (2 ozs.) Lime juice
30 gms. Almonds blanched and shredded
30 gms. Pistachios blanched and shredded

30 gms. Charoli, blanched, whole
30 gms. Raisins, cut into halves
240 mls. (8 ozs.) Milk
30 mls. (1 oz.) Kewada water

A good pinch of Saffron diluted in warm water
15 gms. Coconut grated
60 gms. Ghee
60 gms. Onions, thinly and evenly sliced.

● **Prepare** *yakhni* **as follows:** Boil meat in water along with all the ingredients for *yakhni*. When meat is tender, remove from the liquid and keep

* *Picture on page 124.*

aside. Strain the liquid through a muslin squeezing spices well to extract maximum flavour. The quantity of the liquid should be 6 cups. Cook extra if more, add water if less.

- Heat the ghee and boiled meat along with salt, red chillies, curd and ginger, and brown it lightly. Add coriander seeds, Panjabi badi, and *garam masala* powder, and stir. Add a tablespoonful of water and simmer on low heat till water dries up.
- Wash and soak rice in deep water for half an hour.
- In a separate pan put *yakhni*. When it starts boiling, add rice along with salt and ghee. Cover and cook on medium heat. When three-fourths cooked, put on hot ashes and some live charcoals on top of the lid and simmer till the liquid dries up.
- In a separate pan boil minced meat in about 4 cups of water along with split grams. When tender, dry water completely. Add salt, red chillies and khoa. Grind the meat finely. Divide into 20 equal parts. Flatten, wetting hands with a little water to give kababs a smooth and even shape. Deep fry them in ghee to a golden brown. Cool a bit. Wrap them with silver varak. Keep aside.
- Grease a heavy-bottomed pan with a little ghee. Put half of the meat spreading evenly. Spread one-fourth of rice over the meat. Mix together almonds, pistachios, charoli, raisins and coconut, and spread half of this mixture over the rice. Then sprinkle half of the sugar and half of the lime juice. Cover with one-fourth rice. Repeat this process. After final layer of rice sprinkle saffron. Add kewada water to the milk and sprinkle over the rice.
- Heat the ghee and fry sliced onions to a golden brown. Add ghee along with fried onions to the rice.
- Put a wet cloth over the rice covering it completely.
- Put on *dum* for half an hour. When serving, decorate rice with kababs.

Paya ka Soyta

Preparation time: 1 hour • Cooking time: 2 hours • To serve: 8 – 10 persons.

1 kg. Trotters dresssed and cut into 2" pieces (Roughly 8 average trotters)

½ kg. Rice

250 gms. Ghee

115 gms. Onions thinly and evenly sliced

6 Cloves whole

4 Black cardamoms whole

2 2" Cinnamon sticks whole

2 Bay leaves whole

250 gms. Curd

36 gms. Salt

25 gms. Red chillies powdered

6 gms. Cumin seeds whole

6 gms. Turmeric

50 gms. Garlic ground

15 mls. (½ oz.) Lime juice

1 tbsp. Fresh coriander leaves chopped.

• Clean the trotters by dipping them in boiling water and scraping away hair and deposits with a knife. Keep on repeating this process till the trotters are absolutely clean. While doing so take care in not cutting away the skin. Cut them into 2" pieces. Cleaned trotters are also available at most of the butcher shops.

• Boil the trotter pieces in water till they are absolutely tender. This will take a couple of hours.

• Alternatively, boil them in a pressure cooker with 6 cups of water at 15 lbs. pressure for 45 minutes.

• Wash and soak the rice in water for an hour.

• Heat the ghee and fry sliced onions to a golden brown. Remove, grind and keep aside. In the ghee add cloves, black cardamoms, cinnamon and bay leaves. After a while add curd, salt, red chillies, cumin seeds, turmeric and garlic, and *bhunao* till well-browned and ghee separates from the *masala*.

• Add boiled trotters along with the water in which the trotters were boiled. Add fried ground onions and stir. Cook for 15 minutes.

• Add rice and stir. The liquids should be 1½" above the surface level of the rice. For that add more water if necessary. Cover and cook. Stir occasionally. When rice is half cooked, add lime juice and fresh coriander leaves, and stir. Reduce the heat to the minimum and put some live charcoals on top of the lid. Simmer till rice is well-cooked and the liquids dry up completely.

Hareesa Badshahi

Preparation time: 1 hour ● Cooking time: 2 hours ● To serve: 8 – 10 persons.

½ kg. Wheat whole (preferably Khandwa variety)

2½ litres Milk

1 kg. Lean mutton from leg *or* shoulder

250 gms. Ghee

36 gms. Red chillies powdered

18 gms. Coriander seeds powdered

6 gms. Cumin seeds powdered

3 gms. Ani seeds powdered

25 gms. Onions ground

18 gms. Garlic ground

18 gms. Ginger scraped and ground

30 gms. Salt

3 gms. Cardamom seeds powdered

250 gms. Ghee for *baghar*

40 Cloves whole.

● Prepare the pounded wheat as described in Recipe No. 99.

● Boil milk in a pan. Add pounded wheat and cook for an hour stirring regularly taking care that it does not stick to the bottom of the pan. Keep on adding water as necessary. When very soft and pulpy, remove from fire. Strain through a sieve and keep aside.

● Prepare *yakhni* as follows: In a separate pan boil meat in water along with ghee, red chillies, coriander seeds, cumin seeds, ani seeds, onions, garlic and ginger. When meat is tender, remove from the liquid. Shred the meat pieces into thin fibres and keep aside. Strain the liquid through a muslin, squeezing spices well to extract maximum flavour. The quantity of the liquid should be about 3 cups. Cook extra if water is more, add water if less. In a pan boil *yakhni*, add wheat pulp and salt. Cook on low fire stirring regularly. When it starts thickening, add meat and mix well. When it thickens and begins to come off the sides of the pan, add cardamom powder. In a separate pan heat the ghee for *baghar* and add cloves. When they turn dark brown add ghee, along with cloves, to the pan and stir well.

Santh Bajre ka Soyta

Preparation time: 1 hour • Cooking time: 2 hours • To serve: 8 – 10 persons.

½ kg. Fresh pig skin with fat. Cut into 1½"×1½" pieces	18 gms. Garlic ground	60 gms. Ghee for millet
	18 gms. Ginger scraped and ground	5 Cloves whole
175 gms. Millet (Bajra) pounded	2 2" Cinnamon sticks coarsely powdered	18 gms. Salt
60 gms. Split green beans (Moong dal) skinless	2 Black cardamoms coarsely powdered	60 gms. Ghee for pig skin
9 gms. Red chillies powdered	8 Pepper corns coarsely powdered	30 gms. Onions thinly and evenly sliced
18 gms. Coriander seeds powdered	1½ gms. Black cumin seeds coarsely powdered	3 gms. Red chillies powdered
28 gms. Onions ground	1 cup Milk	1½ gms. Garam masala powder
		60 gms. Curd.

- Prepare and boil pig skin as described in Recipe No. 81.
- Moisten the millet with a little water and keep for half an hour. Then pound it lightly just breaking each grain into two. Put in a sieve and stir, removing and discarding over-pounded grains turned into powder.
- Soak the pounded millet in deep water for a while. Stir and drain water which will remove chaff and impurities. Wash split green beans thoroughly.
- Prepare *yakhni* as follows: Boil red chillies, coriander seeds, onions, garlic, ginger, cinnamon, black cardamoms, pepper corns and black cumin seeds with 4 cups of water for 15 minutes. Strain the liquid through muslin. Add milk and keep aside.
- Heat the ghee in a large pan (to avoid frothing over). Add cloves, when they turn dark brown add enough water to cook the millet. When it starts boiling add millet and split green beans. Add salt. Cover and cook. When half-cooked, add *yakhni*. Keep on stirring till millet is well-cooked and of thick consistency.
- In a separate pan heat ghee and fry sliced onions to a golden brown. Remove and keep aside. In the same ghee add boiled pig skin along with red chillies, *garam masala* powder and curd and put on *dum* till the liquid dries up completely.
- Add pig skin and fried onions to the millet and mix well. Put on low fire till ghee films on the surface.
- In the above recipe trotters may be used instead of pig skin.

Hareesa Rashmi

Preparation time: 1 hour ● Cooking time: 2 hours ● To serve: 8 – 10 persons.

½ kg. Wheat whole (preferably Khandwa variety)
½ kg. Mutton pieces
115 gms. Ghee for mutton
25 gms. Garlic ground
25 gms. Ginger scraped and ground
30 gms. Salt
3 gms. Red chillies powdered

6 gms. Coriander seeds, powdered
3 gms. Turmeric
3 gms. Cumin seeds whole
6 gms. *Garam masala* powder
25 gms. Green chillies chopped finely without seeds

1 tbsp. Fresh mint leaves chopped finely
30 mls. (1 oz.) Lime juice
115 gms. Pure ghee for hareesa
115 gms. Onions thinly and evenly sliced
12 gms. Ginger scraped and chopped finely.

● Soak the wheat in deep water for 24 hours. Then spread on clean cloth to dry for about half an hour. Pound till the outer skin is removed. Discard chaff. This should be done in advance to save cooking time.

● Heat the ghee and fry together garlic and ginger to a golden brown. Add meat along with salt, red chillies, coriander seeds, turmeric and cumin seeds. *Bhunao* the meat to a light brown colour. Add water and stir. Cover and cook till tender. Add pounded wheat and hot water. Cook on medium heat for about an hour, stirring regularly taking care that it does not stick to the bottom of the pan. Keep on adding water as necessary till it is soft and pulpy. When the mixture thickens and begins to come off the sides of the pan, add *garam masala* powder, green chillies, mint leaves and lime juice, and stir well. Remove from fire and keep on hot ashes.

● In a separate pan heat the ghee and fry sliced onions to a golden brown. Remove and keep aside.

● Just before meals, serve hareesa in a dish. Sprinkle fried onions and chopped ginger over it. Reheat the ghee and pour over the haressa. Do not stir.

100

Sewian ki Biryani*

Preparation time: 1 hour • Cooking time: 2 hours • To serve: 8 – 10 persons.

250 gms. Minced lean mutton from leg *or* shoulder (*Keema*)
60 gms. Ghee for mutton
60 gms. Onions thinly and evenly sliced
3 gms. Salt
60 gms. Curd
6 gms. Coriander seeds powdered
6 gms. Ginger scraped and ground

6 gms. *Garam masala* powder
1½ gms. Ani seeds powdered
15 mls. (½ oz.) Kewada water
A good pinch of Saffron diluted in warm water
115 gms. Fresh green peas shelled

50 gms. Ghee for peas
3 gms. Salt for peas
1½ gms. Sugar for peas
250 gms. Vermicelli
115 gms. *Malai*
12 gms. Salt
½ litre Milk
60 gms. Ghee for vermicelli.

• In a heavy-bottomed pan heat the ghee and fry sliced onions to a golden brown. Add minced meat and salt, and stir. Cover and cook till the meat juices dry up. Add water and cook. When tender and water dries up completely, add curd, coriander seeds, ginger, *garam masala* powder and ani seeds, and stir. Put on *dum* till the liquid dries up completely. Add kewada water and saffron. Keep aside.

• In a separate pan cook peas along with ghee, salt and sugar with so much water that it dries up when peas are tender but not mushy. Spread peas over the meat. Spread half of the vermicelli evenly over the peas. Sprinkle *malai*, then spread remaining half of the vermicelli. Add salt to the milk and heat it well. Sprinkle milk over the vermicelli.

• Put an iron *tawa* or a thick metal plate on medium fire. On this place the pan. This indirect heat would safeguard the vermicelli sticking to the bottom of the pan. Simmer this way for half an hour. Do not put live charcoals on lid.

• Heat the ghee and sprinkle over the vermicelli. Stir gently blending meat and vermicelli evenly. Then reduce the heat to the minimum and keep on for another half an hour.

* Picture on page 124.

101

Hareesa Adas

Preparation time: 1 hour • Cooking time: 2 hours • To serve: 8 – 10 persons.

750 gms. Lean mutton from leg or shoulder
12 gms. Coriander seeds coarsely ground
12 gms. Cumin seeds coarsely ground
12 gms. Ani seeds coarsely ground
115 gms. Onions ground
18 gms. Garlic ground
½ kg. Lentils red (Masoor dal)

60 gms. Rice
60 gms. Curd
115 gms. Ghee for baghar
5 Cloves whole
25 gms. Salt
18 gms. Ginger scraped and ground
9 gms. Cinnamon powdered
240 mls. (8 ozs.) Milk

115 gms. Malai
15 Cloves powdered
250 gms. Ghee for hareesa
50 gms. Almonds blanched and shredded
25 gms. Pistachios blanched and shredded.

• Boil meat in water along with coriander seeds, cumin seeds, ani seeds, onions and garlic. When meat is tender, remove from liquid. Shred the meat into thin fibres and keep aside. Strain the liquid through a muslin, squeezing spices well to extract maximum flavour. The quantity of the liquid should be 3 cups. Cook extra if water is more, add water if less.

• Wash the lentils thoroughly. Cook in about 4 cups of water. Keep aside.

• In a separate pan cook rice with one cup of water. Add rice to the lentils. Add curd and yakhni and stir well. Strain through a sieve. Heat the ghee for baghar and add cloves, when they turn dark brown add ghee, along with cloves to the above mixture. Add salt.

• Extract ginger juice through a muslin. Add ginger juice and half of the cinnamon powder to the meat and mix well. Add meat to the above mixture. Add milk and malai and stir well. Cook on low fire stirring regularly. When it thickens and begins to come off the sides of the pan, add remaining half of the cinnamon powder and clove powder and mix well.

• In a separate pan heat the ghee and add to the mixture and stir. Add almonds and pistachios and put on dum for 15 minutes.

Sewian Pulao

Preparation time: 1 hour • Cooking time: 2 hours • To serve: 8 – 10 persons.

Ingredients for Boiling Mutton

½ kg. Mutton pieces	1½ gms. Ani seeds coarsely ground	1½ gms. Red chillies powdered
2 Black cardamoms coarsely ground	2 Bay leaves	25 gms. Onions ground
20 Pepper corns coarsely ground	A good pinch of mace ground	6 gms. Garlic ground
5 Cloves coarsely ground	3 gms. Coriander seeds powdered	6 gms. Ginger scraped and ground.
2 2″ Cinnamon sticks coarsely ground		

Ingredients for *Bhunao* Meat

60 gms. Ghee for mutton	A good pinch of Asafoetida diluted in water	6 gms. Panjabi badi powdered
6 gms. Salt		A good pinch of Saffron diluted in warm water.
3 gms. Red chillies powdered	175 gms. Curd	
12 gms. Ginger scraped and ground	12 gms. Coriander seeds powdered	

Ingredients for Layers

250 gms. Vermicelli	240 mls. (8 ozs.) Milk	60 gms. Onions thinly and evenly sliced
250 gms. Ghee for frying vermicelli	12 gms. Salt for *yakhni*	
	60 gms. Ghee for vermicelli	15 mls. (½ oz.) Rose water.

• Prepare *yakhni* as follows: Boil meat in water along with all the ingredients in this section. When meat is tender, remove from the liquid and keep aside. Strain the liquid through a muslin squeezing spices well to extract maximum flavour. The quantity of liquid should be 6 cups. Cook extra if water is more or add water if less.

• In a heavy-bottomed pan heat the ghee. Add boiled meat along with salt, red chillies, ginger and asafoetida. *Bhunao* the meat adding curd a little at a time. Add coriander seeds, Panjabi badi and saffron and half cup water, and stir. Put on *dum* till liquid dries up completely.

• In a *kadhai* heat the ghee and fry vermicelli on very low heat to a golden colour. Remove from ghee and spread over the meat evenly. Add milk and salt to the *yakhni* and heat it well on fire. Sprinkle it over the vermicelli.

- Put an iron *tawa* or a thick metal plate on medium fire. On this place the pan. This indirect heat would safeguard the vermicelli sticking to the bottom of the pan. Simmer this way for half an hour. Do not put live charcoals on lid.
- Heat the ghee and fry sliced onions to a golden brown. Remove and spread over the vermicelli. In the same ghee add rose water and sprinkle over the vermicelli. Stir very gently blending meat and vermicelli evenly. Then reduce the heat to the minimum and keep for another half an hour.

103

Sailana Dal

Preparation time: 30 minutes • Cooking time: 1 hour • To serve: 6 – 8 persons.

½ kg. Yellow lentils (*Toovar dal*)	30 gms. Salt	25 gms. Green chillies whole
250 gms. Ghee	9 gms. Red chillies powdered	6 gms. Cumin seeds powdered
18 gms. Garlic chopped	3 gms. Turmeric	45 mls. (1½ ozs.) Lime juice
A piece of Asafoetida the size of pepper corn diluted in water	1½ gms. Soda bi-carbonate	2 tbsps. Fresh coriander leaves chopped.
	12 gms. Molasses	

• Heat the ghee and fry chopped garlic to a golden brown. Add asafoetida and enough water to cook lentils. When it starts boiling, add lentils along with salt, red chillies, turmeric, soda bi-carbonate, molasses and green chillies. Cover and cook. When cooked, it should be of thick consistency. Add cumin seeds, lime juice and coriander leaves, and stir.

104

Banjari Dal*

Preparation time: 30 minutes • Cooking time: 1 hour • To serve: 6 – 8 persons.

½ kg. Split black beans (*Urad dal*)	250 gms. Green chillies chopped, finely with seeds	125 gms. Ginger scraped and chopped finely
250 gms. Ghee		30 gms. Salt.

• Wash and soak black beans in deep water for 8 to 12 hours. Stir with hand and remove skin of the beans completely. Just before cooking drain out the water completely.
• Put beans in a pan. Add only as much water that it should be two inches above the beans. Cover and cook on low fire. If necessary more water may be added afterwards. When half-cooked, add green chillies, ginger and salt, and stir. When cooked, add ghee and put on *dum*, and keep on stirring lightly till it gets thick consistency.

* *Picture on page 157.*

136

Dal Be Aab (Dal Without Water)

I am grateful to His Late Highness Maharajadhiraj Harisinghji of Kashmir for giving me this fine recipe.

Preparation time: 30 minutes ● Cooking time: 2 hours ● To serve: 6 – 8 persons.

½ kg. Split green beans (*Moong dal*) skinless	12 gms. Red chillies whole	25 gms. Coriander seeds powdered
½ kg. Ghee	36 gms. Salt	12 gms. Ginger scraped and ground.
½ kg. Onions thinly and evenly sliced	6 gms. Black cumin seeds powdered	
	3 gms. Cardamom seeds powdered	

● Wash and soak split green beans in deep water for 8 to 10 hours. Just before cooking drain out the water completely. Mix salt into the beans. Heat the ghee. Add red chillies whole, when they turn black remove the ghee from fire, and cool a bit.

● Mix thoroughly all the remaining ingredients into the sliced onions. Spread the onions evenly over the ghee. Then over the onions spread the beans evenly. Do not stir. No water to be added.

● Close the pan with tight lid and seal the edges of the lid with wheat flour paste. On a low heat cook for an hour and a half. Before serving take the beans into a separate pan without onions (which are to be discarded) and stir well blending beans with the ghee.

Dal Panchratan

Preparation time: 30 minutes • Cooking time: 1 hour • To serve: 6 – 8 persons.

100 gms. Yellow lentils (*Toovar dal*)	
100 gms. Red lentils (*Masur dal*)	
100 gms. Split grams (*Chana dal*)	
100 gms. Split green beans (*Moong dal*) skinless	
100 gms. Split black beans (*Urad dal*) skinless	
250 gms. Ghee	

115 gms. Onions thinly and evenly sliced
40 gms. Salt
18 gms. Red chillies powdered
18 gms. Coriander seeds powdered
9 gms. Turmeric
115 gms. Onions ground
25 gms. Garlic ground

25 gms. Ginger scraped and ground
25 gms. Green chillies chopped with seeds
9 gms. Cumin seeds coarsely powdered
3 gms. *Garam masala* powder
30 mls. (1 oz.) Lime juice
1 tbsp. Fresh coriander leaves chopped.

• Heat the ghee and fry sliced onions to a golden brown. Add salt, red chillies, coriander seeds, turmeric, onions, garlic and ginger. *Bhunao* till the *masala* is well-browned and ghee separates from it.

• Add water. When it starts boiling add split grams and split black beans. Cover and cook. After 15 minutes add the remaining lentils, green chillies and cumin seeds. Cover and cook. When cooked, it should be of thick consistency. Add *garam masala*, lime juice and chopped coriander leaves, and stir.

107

Dal Urad

½ kg. Split black beans (*Urad dal*)
120 gms. Ghee
1½ gms. Soda bi-carbonate
18 gms. Salt
240 mls. (8 ozs.) Milk
15 gms. Ginger scraped and ground

15 gms. Red chillies powdered and roasted dry
10 Cloves powdered
2 2" Cinnamon sticks powdered
4 Cardamoms powdered
10 Pepper corns powdered

1½ gms. Cumin seeds powdered
120 gms. Ghee for *baghar*
60 gms. Onions thinly and evenly sliced
A good pinch of Asafoetida powdered.

● Wash and soak black beans in deep water for 8 to 12 hours. Stir with hand and remove skin of the beans completely. Drain water.

● Heat the ghee and fry beans to a golden colour. Add enough water as to cook the beans. Add soda bi-carbonate. When cooked, add salt and milk, and cook till it is of thick consistency. Add ginger, red chillies, cloves, cinnamon, cardamoms, pepper corns and cumin seeds and stir. Remove from fire.

● Heat the ghee for *baghar* and fry onions to a golden brown. Add asafoetida and give *baghar* to the beans. Mix well.

Khatte Moong Sabat*

Preparation time: 15 minutes ● Cooking time: 30 minutes ● To serve: 8 – 10 persons.

½ kg. Green beans (*Moong* whole) green variety
115 gms. Ghee
3 gms. Red chillies whole
A pinch of Asafoetida diluted in water

30 gms. Salt
6 gms. Red chillies powdered
6 gms. Cumin seeds whole
3 gms. Turmeric

18 gms. Ginger scraped and shredded
½ kg. Curd thick and well beaten
60 gms. Mustard (*Rai*) whole.

● Grind mustard finely in a little water; add salt and keep it for 12 hours before using it.

● Heat the ghee. Add red chillies whole, when they turn black add asafoetida, and then enough water to cook the beans. When the water starts boiling add beans along with red chillies, cumin seeds, turmeric and ginger. Cover and cook. When cooked, water should almost be dry. Remove from fire.

● In a separate pan add mustard paste with salt into the curd and mix well. Add this curd into the beans, and stir gently so that the beans remain intact and may not become mushy. Serve at once. Not to be reheated.

Picture on page 157.

Kadhi Kashmiri

Preparation time: 30 minutes • Cooking time: 1 hour • To serve: 8 – 10 persons.

Ingredients for Kadhi

60 gms. Gram flour (*Besan*)
4 cups Sour buttermilk
  or
120 gms. Sour curd diluted in 4 cups of water and well beaten
15 gms. Salt

1½ gms. Red chillies powdered
1½ gms. Turmeric
1½ gms. Cumin seeds whole
  A pinch of Asafoetida diluted in water
6 gms. Sugar

18 gms. Fresh mint leaves (*Hara podina*)
25 gms. Green chillies chopped without seeds
15 gms. Mustard oil.

Ingredients for Pakoras

115 gms. Gram flour (*Besan*) for pakoras
6 gms. Salt
3 gms. Red chillies powdered

3 gms. Cumin seeds whole
1½ gms. Soda bi-carbonate or baking powder

A pinch of Asafoetida diluted in water
Mustard oil for deep frying pakoras.

• Mix gram flour in the buttermilk and stir till all lumps disappear. Add salt, red chillies, turmeric, cumin seeds and asafoetida and about 8 cups of water. In a separate pan heat the mustard oil. When it becomes smoking hot, add the above *kadhi* mixture, and keep on stirring till it starts boiling. Then cover and cook on low heat. After half an hour add sugar, mint leaves and green chillies, and cook for another 15 minutes. It should be like thick soup. If necessary hot water may be added to get this consistency.

• In a separate pan put gram flour, for pakora along with salt, red chillies, cumin seeds, soda bi-carbonate and asafoetida. Add a little warm water and mix well. Add more water as necessary, till it becomes a thick batter. Heat the oil in a *kadhai*. When it becomes smoking hot, remove from fire and cool a bit. Put again on fire. Deep fry the pakoras, of medium size, on a medium heat till golden brown.

• Add the pakoras to the *kadhi* and stir. Keep on hot ashes till the pakoras become soft.

110

Bathwa ki Kadhi

Preparation time: 30 minutes • Cooking time: 1 hour • To serve: 6 – 8 persons.

250 gms. Bathwa leaves finely chopped
60 gms. Fresh peas *or* fresh grams (optional)
18 gms. Sesame oil (*Til ka tel*)
6 gms. Garlic chopped
15 gms. Gram flour (*Besan*)

60 gms. Sour curd diluted in 2 cups of water and well beaten
30 mls. (1 oz.) Lime juice
9 gms. Salt
3 gms. Red chillies powdered
1½ gms. Turmeric

3 gms. Cumin seeds whole
30 gms. Onions ground
12 gms. Garlic ground
12 gms. Green chillies chopped with seeds.

● Mix gram flour in curd and stir till all lumps disappear. Add salt, red chillies, turmeric, cumin seeds, onions, garlic and green chillies; mix well.
● Heat the oil. When it becomes smoking hot, remove from fire and cool a bit and put again on fire. Fry chopped garlic to a golden brown. Add the above gram flour mixture, bathwa, peas and about 4 cups of water and cook on medium heat stirring till it starts boiling. When cooked, it should be of thick consistency.
● Give *dhungar*, method No.1.

111
Palak Dahi*

Preparation time: 30 minutes ● Cooking time: 1 hour ● To serve: 6 – 8 persons.

½ kg. Spinach
60 gms. Onions thinly and evenly sliced
60 gms. Ghee
12 gms. Ginger scraped and ground
12 gms. Salt
1½ gms. Cloves powdered

1½ gms. Cinnamon powdered
1½ gms. Black cardamoms powdered
½ kg. Curd fresh and thick
12 gms. Rice roasted dry and powdered

12 gms. Garlic ground
6 gms. Salt for curd
60 gms. Ghee for *baghar*
1½ gms. Cloves whole for *baghar*.

● Wash the spinach and cut it finely.

● Heat the ghee and fry sliced onions to a golden brown. Add spinach and ginger. Add about one cup of water and cook on moderate heat. When cooked, dry the water completely. Add salt, cloves, cinnamon and black cardamoms and stir. Keep aside.

● Beat the curd well and add rice powder, garlic and salt. Mix thoroughly.

● In a separate pan heat the ghee for *baghar*. Add cloves when they turn dark brown put the ghee, with cloves, into the curd. Then add spinach into the curd and mix well. Serve at once. Not to be reheated.

* Picture on page 157.

Dum Alu

Preparation time: 30 minutes • Cooking time: 1 hour • To serve: 6 – 8 persons.

½ kg. Potatoes round and of walnut size	60 gms. Curd	30 gms. Khoa ground
250 gms. Ghee for frying potatoes	12 gms. Salt	3 gms. Panjabi badi powdered
30 gms. Onions thinly and evenly sliced	9 gms. Red chillies powdered	1½ gms. *Garam masala* powder
12 gms. Ginger scraped and ground	9 gms. Coriander seeds powdered	1 tbsp. Fresh coriander leaves chopped.
	1½ gms. Cumin seeds powdered	

- Boil potatoes in water. When half-cooked, remove, peel and prick well with a tooth-pick.
- Heat the ghee in a *kadhai* and fry the potatoes on strong fire. When potatoes become a bit firm, sprinkle a teaspoonful of water over them. Repeat this process thrice at a little interval. This will help ghee to penetrate into the potatoes. When potatoes become golden brown, remove and keep aside.
- Reduce ghee to 115 gms. Fry sliced onions to a golden brown, remove, grind and keep aside.
- In the same ghee add ginger and brown it. Add curd and stir well. Add salt, red chillies, coriander seeds, cumin seeds and khoa, and *bhunao* till dark brown. Add about 2 cups of water and stir. When it starts boiling, add potatoes, cover and cook on low fire. When cooked and very little water remains, add fried onions, Panjabi badi, *garam masala* powder and coriander leaves. Put on *dum* till water dries completely.

113
Alu ka Rajai Salan

Preparation time: 30 minutes • Cooking time: 1 hour • To serve: 6 – 8 persons.

½ kg. Potatoes large
115 gms. Ghee
60 gms. Onions thinly and evenly sliced
6 gms. Turmeric
12 gms. Salt

6 gms. Red chillies powdered
6 gms. Coriander seeds powdered
1½ gms. Pepper corns powdered

3 gms. Cardamoms powdered
3 gms. Cloves powdered
115 gms. Curd.

• Peel the potatoes and cut into halves lengthwise. Prick with a tooth-pick.
• Heat the ghee in a *kadhai* and fry sliced onions to a golden brown, remove and crush finely and keep aside.
• In the same ghee add turmeric and stir it till dark brown. Strain the ghee through muslin and discard turmeric.
• Heat the same ghee and fry potatoes on low fire till golden brown. Remove and keep aside.
• In the same ghee add salt, red chillies, coriander seeds, pepper corns, cardamoms and cloves, and *bhunao* them twice. Add potatoes, fried onions and curd, and put on *dum* till potatoes become tender.
• No water to be added.

114

Ratalu Rajwadi

Preparation time: 30 minutes • Cooking time: 1 hour • To serve: 6 – 8 persons.

½ kg. Yam (*Ratalu*) peeled and cut into 1" thick round pieces
115 gms. Ghee
15 gms. Salt

12 gms. Red chillies powdered
12 gms. Coriander seeds powdered
12 gms. Kachri powdered

3 gms. Cumin seeds whole
3 gms. Turmeric
60 gms. Onions ground
25 gms. Garlic ground.

• Prick the yam pieces well with a fork.
• Heat the ghee and add all the ingredients; *bhunao* till well-browned and ghee separates from the *masala*. Add yam and *bhunao* thrice.
• Add about 2 cups of water and cook on low heat. When tender, dry the liquids completely.
• Give *dhungar*, method No. 3.

Arvi Rogani

Preparation time: 1 hour • Cooking time: 1½ hours • To serve: 6 – 8 persons.

½ kg. Colocasia (*Arvi*) even sized and peeled
12 gms. Salt in water for soaking colocasia
250 gms. Ghee
60 gms. Onions thinly and evenly sliced

12 gms. Salt
12 gms. Red chillies powdered
12 gms. Coriander seeds powdered
3 gms. Cumin seeds powdered

3 gms. Pepper corns powdered
3 gms. *Garam masala* powder
6 gms. Ginger scraped and ground
115 gms. Curd.

• Peel the colocasia and cut into halves, lengthwise. Prick well with a tooth-pick. Add salt in about 4 cups of water and soak colocasia in it for half an hour. Take out and wash well with fresh water twice. Wipe out the moisture with a cloth.

• Heat the ghee in a *kadhai* and fry colocasia on low fire till golden brown, remove and keep aside.

• In the same ghee fry sliced onions to a golden brown. Remove and grind.

• In the same ghee, add fried colocasia, fried ground onions, and all the remaining ingredients and stir.

• Cover and put on *dum* till the liquids dry up completely. Raw bananas can be cooked in the same way.

Dum Arvi

Preparation time: 1 hour • Cooking time: 2 hours • To serve: 6 – 8 persons.

½ kg. Colocasia (*Arvi*) even sized
Mustard oil for deep frying colocasia
115 gms. Ghee for *masala*
60 gms. Onions thinly and evenly sliced
115 gms. Curd
12 gms. Salt
6 gms. Red chillies powdered

6 gms. Coriander seeds powdered
3 gms. Cumin seeds whole
3 gms. Turmeric
60 gms. Onions ground
12 gms. Garlic ground
12 gms. Ginger scraped and ground
3 Black cardamoms ground dry

10 Cloves ground dry
2 2″ Cinnamon sticks ground dry
2 Bay leaves ground dry
1½ gms. Black cumin ground dry
1½ gms. Nutmeg (*Jaiphal*) ground dry.

• Boil colocasia in water till tender. Peel and prick well with a fork.
• Heat the mustard oil in a *kadhai*. When smoking hot remove from fire and cool a bit. Put back on fire. Fry colocasia on low heat. When colocasia becomes a bit firm, sprinkle a teaspoonful of water over them. Repeat this process thrice at a little interval. This will help oil to penetrate into the colocasia. When colocasia becomes golden brown, remove and keep aside.
• In a separate pan heat the ghee and fry sliced onions to a golden brown. Add curd, salt, red chillies, coriander seeds, cumin seeds, turmeric, onions, garlic and ginger, and *bhunao* till well-browned and ghee separates from the *masala*. Add about 2 cups of water. When it starts boiling, add colocasia along with all the remaining ingredients. Put on *dum* till colocasia becomes tender and ghee films on the surface of the gravy.

Petha ka Keema

Preparation time: 30 minutes • Cooking time: 1 hour • To serve: 6 – 8 persons.

½ kg. Ash gourd (*Petha*) grated and squeezed
Sesame oil (*Til ka tel*) for deep frying the *petha*
50 gms. Ghee for *masala*
6 gms. Salt

12 gms. Red chillies powdered
6 gms. Coriander seeds powdered
3 gms. Cumin seeds whole

3 gms. Turmeric
25 gms. Onions ground
6 gms. Garlic ground
6 gms. Ginger scraped and ground.

• Wash and cut the ash gourd into big pieces. Cut and discard the inner spongy and seeded part. Grate the pulp through a grater. Squeeze out the juices completely, pressing firmly with hands. Keep juices aside to be used later.

• Heat the oil in a *kadhai*. When smoking hot, remove from fire and cool a bit. Put back on fire. Fry the grated ash gourd, about one-fourth at a time, to a golden colour. Keep aside.

• In a separate pan heat the ghee. Add all the ingredients, and *bhunao* till well-browned. In *bhunao* use ash gourd juices instead of water.

• Add fried ash gourd and stir well. Add one cup of water and simmer uncovered, on low heat till water dries up completely.

118
Ratalu Nawabi

Preparation time: 15 minutes • Cooking time: 30 minutes • To serve: 6 – 8 persons.

½ kg. Yam (*Ratalu*) peeled and cut into 1" thick round pieces
175 gms. Ghee
30 gms. Onions thinly and evenly sliced
115 gms. Curd
12 gms. Salt

12 gms. Red chillies powdered
6 gms. Pepper corns powdered
3 gms. Cumin seeds powdered
3 gms. Black cumin seeds powdered

1½ gms. Cloves powdered
1½ gms. Cinnamon powdered
1½ gms. Cardamom seeds powdered
6 gms. Ginger scraped and ground.

• Wash the yam pieces thoroughly in water. Wipe out the moisture with a cloth.
• Heat the ghee in a *kadhai* and fry the yam on low fire to a golden brown. Remove and keep aside.
• In the same ghee fry sliced onions to a golden brown. Add yam along with all the remaining ingredients, and *bhunao* till well-browned.
• Add about a cup of water. Cover and cook on low heat. When tender, dry up the water completely.

119
Kaddu ka Keema*

Preparation time: 15 minutes • Cooking time: 30 minutes • To serve: 6 – 8 persons.

½ kg. Red pumpkin peeled and cubed
12 gms. Salt
12 gms. Red chillies powdered and roasted dry
9 gms. Coriander seeds powdered and roasted dry

6 gms. Cumin seeds powdered and roasted dry
60 gms. Sesame seeds (*Til*) roasted dry and coarsely ground dry

6 gms. Dried green mango powdered
115 gms. Mustard oil
A grain of Asafoetida of size of a pepper corn, whole for *dhungar*.

• Steam the pumpkin pieces till nicely cooked. Mash them finely. Add salt, red chillies, coriander seeds, cumin seeds, sesame seeds and mango powder, and mix well.
• In a separate pan heat the mustard oil. When it is smoking hot, add little by little, into the pumpkin, stirring all the time.
• Give *dhungar*, method No. 2 of asafoetida.
• Add 60 gms. more oil if to be preserved for a few days.

* Picture on page 175.

Suran ka Salan

Preparation time: 30 minutes ● Cooking time: 1 hour ● To serve: 6 – 8 persons.

½ kg. Elephant's foot yam *(Suran)* peeled and cut into 2"×2" square pieces	115 gms. Curd	60 gms. Onions ground
	12 gms. Salt	25 gms. Garlic ground
115 gms. Ghee	12 gms. Red chillies powdered	12 gms. Ginger scraped and ground
2 Black cardamoms whole	12 gms. Coriander seeds powdered	1½ gms. *Garam masala* powder
6 Cloves whole		
2 2" Cinnamon sticks whole	3 gms. Cumin seeds whole	Mustard oil for deep frying Yam.
2 Bay leaves	3 gms. Turmeric	

● Prick the yam pieces well with a fork. Boil the pieces in water till tender. Drain off the water.

● Heat the mustard oil. When smoking hot, remove from fire and cool a bit. Put back on fire. Fry yam pieces on low heat till golden brown and crisp. Remove and keep aside.

● In a separate pan heat the ghee and add black cardamoms, cloves, cinnamon and bay leaves. Add curd, salt, red chillies, coriander seeds, cumin seeds, turmeric, onions, garlic and ginger. *Bhunao* till well-browned and ghee separates from the *masala*. Add yam pieces, and about 6 cups of water. Cover and cook on low heat till the pieces become tender. When gravy becomes thick and ghee floats on top of it add *garam masala* powder.

● Always use Gujarati yam.

Suran Lukmani

Preparation time: 30 minutes ● Cooking time: 1 hour ● To serve: 6 – 8 persons.

½ kg. Elephant's foot yam (*Suran*) peeled and cut into 2"×2" square pieces

115 gms. Ghee

60 gms. Onions thinly and evenly sliced

3 gms. Turmeric

12 gms. Salt

12 gms. Tamarind pulp diluted in warm water

20 Pepper corns powdered

10 Cloves powdered

1 Black cardamom powdered

1 2" Cinnamon stick powdered.

● Heat the ghee and fry sliced onions to a golden brown. Add turmeric and stir. Add yam and salt, and fry it lightly. Add water and cook covered. When half-cooked, add tamarind pulp. When cooked and a little water remains, add the remaining ingredients and stir.

● Put on *dum* till water dries up completely.

● Always use Gujarati yam.

Katahal Shahi

Preparation time: 30 minutes ● Cooking time: 1 hour ● To serve: 6 – 8 persons.

½ kg. Raw jack fruit (*Katahal*) peeled and cut into pieces
Mustard oil for deep frying the *katahal*
115 gms. Ghee for *masala*
4 Black cardamoms whole
6 Cloves whole
2 2″ Cinnamon sticks whole

2 Bay leaves whole
115 gms. Curd
12 gms. Salt
12 gms. Red chillies powdered
12 gms. Coriander seeds powdered
3 gms. Cumin seeds whole

3 gms. Turmeric
60 gms. Onions ground
12 gms. Garlic ground
12 gms. Ginger scraped and ground
1½ gms. Cardamom seeds powdered.

● Select raw jack fruit. Peel and cut into 2½″×2½″ pieces. While cutting it grease hands and also the knife with a little oil.

● Heat mustard oil in a *kadhai*. When smoking hot, remove from fire and cool a bit. Put back on fire. On medium heat fry the jack fruit pieces, 6–7 at a time, to a golden brown. Remove and keep aside.

● In a separate pan heat the ghee. Add black cardamoms, cloves, cinnamon and bay leaves. After a while add all the remaining ingredients, except cardamom powder, and *bhunao* till well-browned and ghee separates from the *masala*.

● Add fried jack fruit pieces and about 2 cups of water, and stir. Cover and cook on low heat till the jack fruit becomes tender and the liquids dry up completely. Add powdered cardamom.

Baghare Baingan

Preparation time: 30 minutes • Cooking time: 1 hour • To serve: 6 – 8 persons.

½ kg. Brinjals small and round
25 gms. Coconut grated and roasted dry
6 gms. Sesame seeds roasted dry
3 gms. Cumin seeds roasted dry
12 gms. Molasses
12 gms. Peanuts roasted
1 tbsp. Fresh coriander leaves

15 gms. Salt
12 gms. Red chillies powdered and roasted dry
3 gms. Coriander seeds powdered and roasted dry
3 gms. Turmeric roasted dry
6 gms. Ginger scraped and ground

6 gms. Garlic ground
6 gms. Parched grams powdered
1½ gms. *Garam masala* powder
115 gms. Sesame oil
30 gms. Onions finely chopped
12 gms. Tamarind pulp.

• Slit brinjals in fours leaving the stem intact. The brinjals should be whole with deep cuts.

• Soak tamarind pulp in a cup of warm water for a while. Strain and keep aside.

• Grind finely together coconut, sesame seeds, cumin seeds, molasses, peanuts and coriander leaves with a little water. Add salt, red chillies, coriander seeds, turmeric, ginger, garlic, parched grams and *garam masala* powder. Mix well. Fill this into the brinjals. If the stuffing is in excess spread it over the brinjals while cooking.

• Heat the oil. When smoking hot remove from fire and cool a bit. Put back on fire. Fry the brinjals lightly, 3–4 at a time. Keep aside. In the same oil fry the chopped onions to a light golden colour. Add brinjals and tamarind juice. Cover and cook on low heat, stir occasionally taking care in not breaking the brinjals.

• When cooked, dry the liquid completely.

Gobhi Matar

Preparation time: 1 hour • Cooking time: 1 hour • To serve: 6 – 8 persons.

½ kg. Cauliflower cut into big pieces

250 gms. Green peas, fresh and shelled

100 gms. Mustard oil

75 gms. Ghee

6 gms. Red chillies whole

3 gms. Mustard (*Rai*) whole

3 gms. Fenugreek seeds (*Methi dana*) whole

6 gms. Cumin seeds whole

A pinch of Asafoetida diluted in water

18 gms. Salt

9 gms. Red chillies powdered

9 gms. Coriander seeds powdered

3 gms. Turmeric

18 gms. Sugar

18 gms. Ginger scraped and ground

3 gms. Cardamom seeds powdered.

• Heat the mustard oil. When it becomes smoking hot add ghee. Add red chillies whole. When they turn black, add fenugreek seeds and let them splitter. Then add mustard to splitter. Add cumin seeds and asafoetida and then cauliflower and peas along with all the remaining ingredients, and stir. No water to be added.

• Cover and cook on low heat till the vegetables are cooked.

125

Mawa Matar

Preparation time: 30 minutes ● Cooking time: 1 hour ● To serve: 6 – 8 persons.

175 gms. *Khoa* ground
375 gms. Green peas fresh and shelled
115 gms. Ghee
18 gms. Salt

9 gms. Red chillies powdered
9 gms. Coriander seeds powdered
18 gms. Ginger scraped and ground

3 gms. *Garam masala* powder
1 tbsp. Fresh coriander leaves chopped.

● Heat the ghee and fry *khoa* on low fire, stirring constantly, to light golden colour.

● Add one cup of water and stir. When it starts boiling add peas along with salt, red chillies, coriander seeds and ginger. Cook on low fire. Add more water if necessary. When peas are tender and water dries up, remove from fire. Add *garam masala* powder and coriander leaves and stir.

126

Chana Matar

Preparation time: 30 minutes ● Cooking time: 30 minutes ● To serve: 6 – 8 persons.

½ kg. Green grams (*Chana*) fresh and shelled
½ kg. Green peas (*Matar*) fresh and shelled
115 gms. Ghee

25 gms. Salt
12 gms. Red chillies powdered
6 gms. Turmeric
12 gms. Garlic ground

115 gms. Ghee for *baghar*
10 Cloves whole
60 gms. Onions chopped finely.

● Grind green grams to fine paste. Heat the ghee and fry peas lightly. Add ground grams along with salt, red chillies, turmeric and garlic. Add one cup of water and stir well. Cook on low fire to thick consistency.

● In a separate pan heat the ghee for *baghar*. Add cloves, when they turn dark brown, add chopped onions and fry to a golden brown. Put it into main dish, stir well and serve.

127

Alu La Javab*

Preparation time: 30 minutes ● Cooking time: 1 hour ● To serve: 6 – 8 persons.

½ kg. Potatoes large
250 gms. Mustard oil for frying potatoes
9 gms. Salt
6 gms. Red chillies powdered and roasted dry
6 gms. Coriander seeds powdered and roasted dry

6 gms. Cumin seeds powdered and roasted dry
25 gms. Sesame seeds (White *til*), roasted and ground dry
6 gms. Dried green mango powdered *or*
15 mls. (½ oz.) Lime juice

50 gms. Mustard oil for *masala*
A grain of Asafoetida of the size of a pepper corn whole.

● Wash and peel the potatoes. Cut lengthwise into big pieces.
● Heat the oil in a *kadhai*. When smoking hot, remove from fire and cool a bit. Put back on fire. Fry potatoes on medium fire to a golden brown and crisp. Remove and cool a bit. Mix salt, red chillies, coriander seeds, cumin seeds, sesame seeds, and mango powder, add potatoes, and mix well. Add mustard oil. Give *dhungar*, method No. 2 of asafoetida.
● Ideal for travelling. Can be preserved for about a week.

Top: Palak Dahi
Mid-left: Alu La Javab
Mid-right: Khatte Moong Sabat
Bottom: Banjari Dal

Picture on facing page.

Petha ke Kabab*

My father always had requests from vegetarians for some exotic dish. Petha normally associated with a sweet dish was turned spicy in this creation. It is tasty and quite different.

Preparation time: 30 minutes ● Cooking time: 1 hour ● To serve: 6 – 8 persons.

½ kg. Ash gourd (*Petha*) unpeeled and cut into 2½"×2½" pieces
115 gms. Sesame oil for frying the *petha* pieces
50 gms. Sesame oil for cooking the *masala*

6 gms. Garlic chopped
6 gms. Salt
9 gms. Red chillies powdered
1½ gms. Coriander seeds powdered
1½ gms. Turmeric

3 gms. Cumin seeds whole
25 gms. Onions ground
6 gms. Garlic ground
1 tbsp. Fresh coriander leaves chopped.

● Wash and cut the ash gourd into 2½"×2½" pieces. Do not peel the skin, as it maintains the shape of the pieces. Cut and discard the inner spongy and seeded part. Give four cuts, crosswise to the pieces, deep upto the skin without cutting it. With a knife puncture the back of the skin at three-four places.

● Heat the oil in *kadhai*. When smoking hot remove from fire and cool a bit. Put back on fire. Fry ash gourd pieces 4–5 at a time, on medium heat till well-browned. Remove and keep aside.

● Heat the oil and fry chopped garlic to a golden brown. Add all the remaining ingredients, except coriander leaves. *Bhunao* till well-browned and ghee separates from the *masala*.

● Add fried ash gourd pieces and stir well. Add 2 cups of water, cover and simmer on low heat till the water dries up completely. Add fresh coriander leaves.

Above: Petha ke Kabab being fried
Below: Finished look

* *Picture on facing page.*

Karela Nafees

Preparation time: 1 hour • Cooking time: 1 hour • To serve: 6 – 8 persons.

250 gms. Bitter gourds (*Karela*) scraped and seeded

250 gms. Onions thinly and evenly sliced

115 gms. Ghee

12 gms. Red chillies powdered

12 gms. Coriander seeds powdered

6 gms. Turmeric

9 gms. Salt

115 gms. Tamarind (*Imli*) flowers *or* 12 gms. tamarind pulp, diluted in warm water

115 gms. Curd

3 gms. *Garam masala* powder

6 gms. Salt for rubbing over the bitter gourds

3 gms. Turmeric for rubbing over the bitter gourds.

• Cut the bitter gourds (*Karela*) into thin and even round pieces. Rub over salt and turmeric and keep for half an hour. This will lessen the bitter flavour. Squeeze them well and wash twice in fresh water, squeezing and removing all the liquid.

• Heat the ghee. Fry sliced onions to a golden brown, remove and keep aside. In the same ghee add red chillies, coriander seeds and turmeric. *Bhunao* twice.

• Add sliced bitter gourds, salt and tamarind flowers and *bhunao* thrice.

• Then add fried onions, curd and *garam masala* powder and stir. Simmer on low fire till the curd dries up completely.

Karela Musallam (Whole)

Preparation time: 1 hour ● Cooking time: $1\frac{1}{2}$ hours ● To serve: 6 – 8 persons.

1 kg. Bitter gourds (*Karela*) long variety, scraped

Mustard oil for frying the bitter gourds

Ingredients for Stuffing

60 gms. Ghee for *masala*

A pinch of Asafoetida, diluted in water

115 gms. Potatoes cut into $\frac{1}{2}$" pieces

115 gms. Split grams (*Chana dal*) boiled and drained

60 gms. Tamarind flowers *or*

6 gms. Tamarind pulp diluted in warm water

6 gms. Ani seeds whole

12 gms. Sugar

12 gms. Salt

6 gms. Red chillies powdered

3 gms. Cumin seeds whole

50 gms. Onions ground

12 gms. Garlic ground

12 gms. Ginger scraped and finely chopped

12 gms. Green chillies finely chopped with seeds

1 tbsp. Fresh coriander leaves finely chopped.

Ingredients for cooking the Gourds

50 gms. Mustard oil for cooking the bitter gourds

60 gms. Curd

6 gms. Salt

6 gms. Red chillies powdered

6 gms. Ginger scraped and ground.

● Scrape the bitter gourds. Boil them in water till half-cooked. Make a slit, lengthwise, in the bitter gourds, and remove the seeds which are to be discarded. Press the *karela* gently with your palms, squeezing out water completely.

● Fry them in mustard oil to a golden colour, remove and keep aside.

● Heat the ghee. Add asafoetida and then potatoes, split grams, tamarind flowers, ani seeds, sugar, salt, red chillies, cumin seeds, onions, garlic, ginger, green chillies and coriander leaves and *bhunao* thrice. Add one cup of water and stir. When cooked, dry the liquids completely cool.

● Stuff the bitter gourds with the above *masala*. Tie a piece of thread around each gourd to prevent the stuffing from running out.

● In a separate pan heat mustard oil and add all the remaining ingredients and stir. Add the stuffed gourds and simmer on low heat till the curd dries up completely. Can be served hot or cold.

Karela-Pyaz*

Preparation time: 1 hour • Cooking time: 1 hour • To serve: 6 – 8 persons.

250 gms. Bitter gourds (Karela) scraped
500 gms. Onions peeled
 25 gms. Salt

12 gms. Red chillies powdered
 6 gms. Cumin seeds powdered

Sesame oil (Til-ka-tel) for deep frying karela and onions.

• Scrape the bitter gourds. Cut into very thin and even round slices with seeds. Mix salt into the sliced bitter gourds and keep for half an hour. Then squeeze thoroughly with hands removing all the liquid. Do not wash.

• Cut the onions into very thin and even round slices.

• Heat the oil in a *kadhai*. When smoking hot remove from fire and cool a bit. Put back on fire. On medium heat, deep fry sliced bitter gourds to a golden brown. Remove and keep aside.

• In the same oil fry sliced onions, half at a time, to a golden brown. Remove and spread them on a wide plate.

• Mix bitter gourds and onions thoroughly but gently, without crushing them. Add red chillies and cumin seeds and mix well.

* Picture on page 175.

Shalgam ka Salan

Preparation time: 1 hour • Cooking time: 1 hour • To serve: 6 – 8 persons.

½ kg. Turnips (*Shalgam*) peeled

6 gms. Salt for applying on turnips

115 gms. Ghee

60 gms. Onions thinly and evenly sliced

12 gms. Salt

12 gms. Red chillies powdered

12 gms. Onions ground

115 gms. Curd

6 gms. Ginger scraped and ground

1½ gms. Dried green mango powdered

3 gms. Coriander seeds powdered

1½ gms. *Garam masala* powder

6 gms. Panjabi badi powdered.

• Peel the turnips and cut into halves. Prick them well with a fork. Rub salt over them and put them in sunlight for half an hour. Wash them well in cold water.

• Heat the ghee and fry sliced onions to a golden brown. Remove and grind. Keep aside.

• In the same ghee add turnips along with salt, red chillies, onions and curd. *Bhunao* thrice. Add water and cook covered on low fire. When cooked and a little water remains add fried onions and all the remaining ingredients. Put on *dum* till ghee floats on top of the gravy.

133
Shalgam ka Bhurta

Preparation time: 30 minutes • Cooking time: 1½ hours • To serve: 6 – 8 persons.

½ kg. Turnips (*Shalgam*) peeled
120 gms. Ghee

6 gms. Salt
6 gms. Red chillies powdered

½ litre Milk
250 gms. Green coconut for extracting milk.

• Cut each turnip into four pieces. Boil them in water. When cooked, drain and discard the water. Grind finely.
• Heat the ghee, add ground turnips along with salt, red chillies and milk. Cook on low fire stirring constantly. When thick, add coconut milk and cook till the liquids dry up completely.

(For extracting coconut milk, first grate it, then grind it finely adding one cup of hot water little at a time. Squeeze through a muslin. Repeat this process to extract maximum milk.)

134
Turai

Preparation time: 30 minutes • Cooking time: 30 minutes • To serve: 6 – 8 persons.

½ kg. Ridge gourds (*Turai*) scraped and cut into 1" pieces
250 gms. Onions cut into 1" pieces

125 gms. Green chillies cut into ½" pieces with seeds
60 gms. Garlic whole

60 gms. Sesame oil
6 gms. Cumin seeds whole
15 gms. Salt.

• Heat the oil. When smoking hot, remove from fire and cool a bit. Put back on fire. Add cumin seeds and then add gourds along with all the ingredients. Cook on low heat, uncovered. No water to be added. Keep on stirring till cooked.
• Parwal, keekoda or gilki can be cooked in the same way.

Kewada

Those who have seen a Kewada flower would never believe that it or parts of it could be eaten. Yet if you follow the recipe you would come with a really unusual vegetarian dish.

Preparation time: 30 minutes ● Cooking time: 1 hour ● To serve: 6 – 8 persons.

250 gms. Spongy portion of Kewada flowers	30 gms. Onions, thinly and evenly sliced	3 gms. Cumin seeds whole
115 gms. Ghee	18 gms. Salt	115 gms. Curd
4 Cloves whole	18 gms. Red chillies powdered	60 gms. Onions ground
1 2″ Cinnamon stick whole		30 gms. Garlic ground
2 Black cardamoms whole	12 gms. Coriander seeds powdered	240 mls. (8 ozs.) Milk
2 Bay leaves whole		30 mls. (1 oz.) Kewada water.

● Select 4/5 fresh kewada flowers. Discard the outer petals. Take out the spongy portion from the centre, keeping them intact. Discard the middle stump. Thrash out pollen dust from them and wash.

● Boil them in plenty of water. When cooked, take out from the water and squeeze well, without breaking them. Discard the water.

● Heat the ghee and add cloves, cinnamon, black cardamoms and bay leaves. After a while add sliced onions and fry till golden brown. Then add salt, red chillies, coriander seeds, cumin seeds, curd, onions and garlic. *Bhunao* till *masala* is well-browned and ghee separates from the *masala*.

● Add kewada along with milk. Simmer on low fire till the milk dries up completely. Add kewada water and stir.

Aam ki Gutli

Eat mangoes and discard the stones, but not always. The stones can be turned into a fine vegetable. They say Mahatma Gandhi always recommended its use.

Preparation time: 1 hour • Cooking time: 1 hour • To serve: 6 – 8 persons.

½ kg. Ripe mango seeds (*Aam ki gutli*) crust removed and sliced
3 gms. Salt for boiling the *gutli*
115 gms. Sesame oil
60 gms. Onions finely chopped

12 gms. Salt
25 gms. Red chillies powdered
3 gms. Cumin seeds whole
3 gms. Turmeric
25 gms. Garlic ground
50 gms. Onions ground

60 gms. Mango pickle *masala*
60 gms. Mango pickle oil.

• Dry the seeds of ripe mangoes in sunlight for a day. Break the hard crust of the seeds and take out the cores.

• Cut the cores into thin slices, 1" long and ½" thick. Boil them along with salt in water till cooked. Take out and wash well in fresh water.

• Heat the oil. When smoking hot, remove from fire and cool a bit. Put back on fire. Fry chopped onions to a golden brown. Add salt, red chillies, cumin seeds, turmeric, garlic and onions, and *bhunao* till well-browned.

• Add boiled cores and *bhunao* twice.

• Add mango pickle *masala*, mango pickle oil and half cup of water and stir. Simmer till the liquids dry up completely and only oil remains. If to be preserved for a few days, add 60 gms. more of sesame oil.

Keekoda (Kantola)

Preparation time: 30 minutes • Cooking time: 30 minutes • To serve: 6 – 8 persons.

½ kg. Keekoda	18 gms. Garlic chopped	9 gms. Salt
250 gms. Onions peeled whole	5 gms. Cumin seeds whole	18 gms. Red chillies powdered.
115 gms. Sesame oil		

• Cut each keekoda into four equal parts, lengthwise. Cut onions into the same size as of the keekoda.

• Heat the oil in a *kadhai*. When it is smoking hot, remove from fire and cool a bit. Put again on fire. Fry chopped garlic to a golden brown. Add cumin seeds. When they splitter, add keekoda and onions; do not cover. Keep on stirring till they are of golden colour. Then add salt and red chillies powdered. Keep on stirring till cooked and well-browned. No water to be used.

138

Goolar (Wild Figs)

Preparation time: 30 minutes • Cooking time: 1 hour • To serve: 6 – 8 persons.

½ kg. Goolar big and raw	18 gms. Salt	12 gms. Dried green mango powdered
A good pinch Asafoetida powdered for boiling goolar	12 gms. Red chillies powdered	A good pinch of Asafoetida
115 gms. Ghee	18 gms. Coriander seeds powdered	3 gms. *Garam masala* powder.
115 gms. Onions thinly and evenly sliced	115 gms. Curd	

• Wash and cut each goolar into four pieces. Boil them in water for five minutes. Drain off the water. Boil them again in fresh water adding asafoetida. When tender, discard the water.

• Heat the ghee and fry sliced onions to a golden brown. Add goolar along with all the remaining ingredients and stir. No water to be added. Cover and cook on low fire, till the curd dries up completely.

Dahi ka Achar

Preparation time: 15 minutes • To serve: 6 – 8 persons.

1 kg. Curd fresh and thick
12 gms. Mustard (*Sarson*) ground with water
3 gms. Salt
1½ gms. Cumin seeds roasted dry and powdered

1½ gms. Black cumin seeds roasted dry and powdered
6 gms. Ginger scraped and ground

A grain of Asafoetida of the size of a pepper corn roasted dry and powdered
60 gms. Mustard oil.

• Put the curd in muslin and hang it on a peg for 4–5 hours. On being drained the curd should be 500 gms. in weight. Grind mustard with water and mix in salt. Keep it for two hours.

• Add ground mustard with salt, cumin seeds, black cumin seeds, ginger and asafoetida to the curd and whip it well. Add mustard oil and mix well. Not to be heated.

• Preferably to be served after 12 hours.

140

Moole Besan

Preparation time: 30 minutes ● Cooking time: 1 hour ● To serve: 6 – 8 persons.

250 gms. Radishes (*Moole*) scraped and cut into ½" pieces
115 gms. Gram flour (*Besan*)
115 gms. Sesame oil
12 gms. Garlic chopped finely

3 gms. Cumin seeds whole
A pinch of Asafoetida diluted in water
12 gms. Salt
12 gms Red chillies powdered

3 gms. Turmeric
50 gms. Onions ground
12 gms. Garlic ground
115 gms. Curd.

● Boil the radishes in about 6 cups of water. When cooked, take out and keep aside. In the same water stir gram flour till all lumps disappear. Keep aside.
● Heat the oil. When smoking hot, remove from fire and cool a bit. Put back on fire. Add chopped garlic and fry till golden brown. Add cumin seeds and then asafoetida. Add all the remaining ingredients. *Bhunao* till well-browned. Add radishes and stir for a while. Add gram flour diluted in water, and cook on low fire, stirring all the time till the mixture stops sticking to the bottom of the pan.

Gur-Amba

Preparation time: 30 minutes • Cooking time: 1 hour • To serve: 6 – 8 persons.

½ kg. Raw mangoes peeled and cut into halves	60 gms. Semolina (*Sujji*)	6 gms. Salt
60 gms. Ghee for frying mangoes	30 gms. Ghee for semolina	30 mls. (1 oz.) Kewada *or* rose water.
	375 gms. Sugar *or* molasses	
	720 mls. Milk	

• Peel the mangoes and discard seeds, cut into halves lengthwise and prick well with tooth pick. Wash the pieces thoroughly in water and wipe out the moisture with a cloth.

• Heat the ghee and fry the mango pieces to a light golden colour. Keep aside.

• Heat the ghee and add semolina. Roast it on low fire stirring constantly till light golden colour.

• Mix sugar and milk. Simmer on fire till the sugar is dissolved. Add semolina and stir well. Add fried mangoes along with ghee in which they were fried. Cook on low fire, stirring regularly, till the mixture is of a very thick consistency. Add kewada or rose water and stir.

• Cool before serving.

142
Aam ke Lonj

Preparation time: 30 minutes • Cooking time: 1 hour • To serve: 6 – 8 persons.

½ kg. Raw mangoes peeled and sliced
50 gms. Ghee
3 gms. Mustard whole
A pinch of Asafoetida diluted in water

12 gms. Salt
9 gms. Red chillies powdered
6 gms. Cumin seeds whole
3 gms. Turmeric

3 gms. Ani seeds coarsely powdered
3 gms. Coriander seeds powdered
250 gms. Sugar.

● Select preferably large sized mangoes. Peel and cut the mangoes into about 1" thick slices. Discard the seeds. Boil the slices in water till half-cooked. Take out the slices and dry them on a paper or cloth.

● Heat the ghee and add mustard; when it splitters add asafoetida. Then add all the ingredients and about 2 cups of water. Keep on stirring till syrup gets one-thread consistency. Add mango slices and simmer on low heat till syrup thickens and the slices become tender and slightly translucent.

Tesu ke Phool (Palash)

Preparation time: $1\frac{1}{2}$ hours • Cooking time: 1 hour • To serve: 4 to 6 persons.

250 gms. Petals of fresh Tesu flowers

125 gms. Sesame oil

25 gms. Garlic chopped

125 gms. Onions cut into 1" pieces

3 gms. Cumin seeds whole

12 gms. Red chillies whole ground coarely

12 gms. Salt

3 gms. Dried green mango powdered.

● Boil petals in water. When tender discard water, squeezing the petals thoroughly.

● Heat the oil, when smoking hot remove from fire and cool a bit. Put back on fire. Fry chopped garlic to golden brown. Add onion pieces and cook till tender. Add cumin seeds and red chillies and stir. Add boiled petals, salt, mango powder and one cup of water and stir. Cook covered on a low heat till water dries up completely.

Dahi Baingan Shirazi

Preparation time: 30 minutes ● Cooking time: 1 hour ● To serve: 6 – 8 persons.

½ kg. Brinjals
12 gms. Salt
60 gms. Ghee
60 gms. Onions thinly and evenly sliced
60 gms. Curd, fresh, thick and well-beaten

12 gms. Ginger scraped and ground and juice extracted
1½ gms. *Garam masala* powder
25 gms. Raisins cut into halves

25 gms. Indian cream cheese (*Panir*) cut into ½" square pieces
25 gms. Green chillies chopped
3 gms. Fresh coriander leaves chopped.

● Steam cook brinjals till tender. Remove skin. Mash the pulp thoroughly with hand. Add salt and keep aside.

● Heat the ghee and fry sliced onions to a golden brown. Remove and keep aside.

● In the same ghee add brinjals and cook for a minute stirring regularly. Remove from fire.

● Add all the remaining ingredients and fried onions, and mix well.

● Give *dhungar*, method No. 2.

● Serve cold.

Baingan ke Lonj*

Preparation time: 1 hour • Cooking time: 1 hour • To serve: 6 – 8 persons.

½ kg. Brinjals long
6 gms. Salt for applying on brinjals
60 gms. Ghee
60 gms. Onions thinly and evenly sliced
12 gms. Red chillies powdered

12 gms. Ginger scraped and chopped finely
5 Cloves powdered
2 2″ Cinnamon sticks powdered
1 Black cardamom powdered
30 Pepper corns powdered

5 Cloves whole
6 gms. Salt
60 gms. Sugar
30 mls. (1 oz.) Lime juice.

● Make a slit, lengthwise, in the brinjals and rub in salt and keep for half an hour.

● Heat the ghee in a *kadhai* and fry sliced onions to a golden brown, remove and crush finely. Mix fried onions, red chillies, ginger and half the quantity of each of cloves, cinnamon, black cardamom and pepper corns.

● Stuff the brinjals with the above *masala*. Tie a piece of thread around each brinjal to prevent the stuffing from running out.

● Heat the above ghee and add cloves whole. When they turn dark brown, add brinjals and salt. Cook on low fire. No water to be added. When cooked, add sugar diluted in lime juice. Put on a *dum* till liquid dries up completely. Add remaining half of the powdered *masalas* and stir gently.

Top: Baingan ke Lonj
Mid-left: Karela Pyaz
Mid-right: Kaddu ka Keema
Bottom: Moong Kabab

* Picture on facing page.

Makki ke Dane No. 1

Preparation time: 30 minutes • Cooking time: 1 hour • To serve: 8 – 10 persons.

½ kg. Fresh corn (*Makka*) kernels grated
115 gms. Ghee
6 gms. Cumin seeds whole
25 gms. Salt
6 gms. Red chillies powdered
12 gms. Coriander seeds powdered

3 gms. Turmeric
50 gms. Onions ground
25 gms. Garlic ground
115 gms. Curd
15 gms. Sugar
60 gms. Gram flour (*Besan*) diluted in water
12 gms. Green chillies finely chopped without seeds

240 mls. Milk
15 mls. (½ oz.) Lime juice
2 tbsps. Fresh coriander leaves chopped.

• Take fresh and tender corns. Grate the kernels but not finely.

• Heat the ghee. Add cumin seeds and then salt, red chillies, coriander seeds, turmeric, onions and garlic, and *bhunao* till well-browned.

• Add grated corn kernels and curd, sugar, gram flour and green chillies and stir. Add enough water to cook the kernels. Cook on medium heat stirring all the time to avoid kernels sticking to the bottom of the pan. When tender and stops sticking to the bottom of the pan, add milk and simmer on low heat till the milk dries up and ghee films on the surface. Add lime juice and chopped coriander leaves and stir well.

Top: Murakkat
Middle: Dahi ka Halwa
Bottom: Dahi ka Bhajia

Makki ke Dane No. 2

Preparation time: 30 minutes • Cooking time: 1 hour • To serve: 8 – 10 persons.

½ kg. Fresh corn (*Makka*) kernels grated
115 gms. Ghee for frying kernels
60 gms. Ghee for *masala*
6 gms. Cumin seeds whole
20 gms. Salt

6 gms. Red chillies powdered
12 gms. Coriander seeds powdered
3 gms. Turmeric
50 gms. Onions ground
25 gms. Garlic ground
115 gms. Curd

12 gms. Sugar
12 gms. Green chillies finely chopped with seeds
15 mls. (½ oz.) Lime juice
2 tbsps. Fresh coriander leaves chopped.

• Take fresh and tender corns. Grate the kernels finely.

• Heat the ghee and fry the corn kernels on low fire. Keep on stirring, to avoid kernels sticking to the bottom of the pan. When golden in colour, remove and keep aside.

• In a separate pan heat the ghee for *masala*. Add cumin seeds and then salt, red chillies, coriander seeds, turmeric, onions, garlic and curd, and *bhunao* till well-browned.

• Add fried kernels, along with the ghee in which they were fried, sugar and chopped green chillies. Add enough water to cook the kernels. Cook on low fire stirring regularly. When tender and stops sticking to the bottom of the pan, add lime juice and chopped coriander leaves, and stir. Remove from fire when the ghee floats on top of the surface.

Dahi ke Kabab

Preparation time: 30 minutes • Cooking time: 1 hour • To serve: 8 – 10 persons.

½ kg. Curd fresh and thick
115 gms. Parched grams powdered
6 gms. Salt for kabab
6 gms. Red chillies powdered for kabab
20 Cloves powdered
3 gms. Cardamoms powdered

1½ gms. Cinnamon powdered
3 gms. Pepper corns powdered
120 gms. Ghee
60 gms. Onions thinly and evenly sliced
6 gms. Salt for *masala*

6 gms. Red chillies powdered for *masala*
12 gms. Garlic ground for *masala*
60 mls. (2 ozs.) Milk.

• Put curd in a muslin and hang it on a peg for 3–4 hours till the liquid drains off completely. On being drained the curd should be 250 gms. in weight.

• Add parched grams, salt and red chillies, and half the quantity of cloves, cardamoms, cinnamon and pepper corns to the curd, and mix well. Divide into 20 equal parts. Flatten, wetting hands with a little water to give the kababs smooth and even shape.

• Heat the ghee in a frying pan and fry the kababs, a few at a time, to a light golden colour. Keep aside.

• In the same ghee, fry the sliced onions to a golden brown, remove and grind and keep aside. In the same ghee add salt, red chillies, garlic, fried ground onions and remaining half of the powdered *masala* and *bhunao* thrice. Add kababs and gently mix into the *masala*. Sprinkle milk on the kababs and remove from the fire and serve at once.

149

Moong Kabab*

Preparation time: 1 hour • Cooking time: 2 hours • To serve: 6 – 8 persons.

250 gms. Split green beans (*Moong dal*)
12 gms. Salt
6 gms. Turmeric
36 gms. Ginger scraped and ground
250 gms. Ghee for frying kababs

1 kg. Curd fresh and thick
15 gms. Salt
60 gms. Ghee for *baghar*
5 Cloves whole for *baghar*
2 2" Cinnamon sticks powdered
2 Black cardamoms powdered

20 Pepper corns powdered
1½ gms. Cumin seeds powdered.

• Wash and soak beans in deep water for 8 to 12 hours. Stir with hand and remove skin of the beans completely. Drain water and grind it to fine paste. Keep 25 gms. of bean paste separately, to be added to the curd.

• Add salt and turmeric to bean paste. Strain ground ginger through a muslin squeezing well to take out the juice. Add this juice to bean paste. Add about 4 cups of water to bean paste. Cook on fire, stirring constantly to avoid sticking it to the bottom of the pan. When the paste begins to solidify, spread it on a greased plate evenly 1" thick. Cool a bit and cut into 4" square pieces. Heat the ghee and fry the pieces to a golden brown.

• Add 25 gms. bean paste, which was kept aside, to curd, and stir well. Sieve curd through a muslin.

• Heat the ghee for *baghar* and add cloves. When they turn dark brown add curd and stir well. When it starts boiling add kababs and remove from fire. Add the remaining ingredients and stir gently. Put on *dum* for 15 minutes.

* Picture on page 175.

150

Hare Chane ke Kabab

Preparation time: 30 minutes • Cooking time: 1 hour • To serve: 6 persons.

½ kg. Green grams (*Chana*) fresh and shelled
18 gms. Salt
6 gms. Coriander seeds powdered
3 gms. Cumin seeds powdered

50 gms. Green chillies ground with seeds
60 gms. Onions ground
25 gms. Garlic ground
115 gms. Curd
25 gms. Ghee for kababs

25 gms. Parched grams powdered
3 gms. Sugar powdered
1½ gms. *Garam masala* powder
Ghee for frying the kababs.

• Boil the grams along with salt, coriander seeds, cumin seeds, green chillies, onions, garlic, curd and ghee in about two cups of water. When cooked, dry the liquids completely. Grind finely, and add the remaining ingredients, mix and knead well.

• Divide into 12 equal parts. Flatten, wetting hands with little water to give the kababs a smooth and even shape.

• In a very little ghee fry on low heat till golden brown.

Goolar Kabab

For vegetarian Kababs, I find these nearest to meat in flavour and texture.

Preparation time: 2 hours • Cooking time: 2 hours • To serve: 10 – 12 persons.

½ kg. Wild figs (*Goolar*) big and raw
115 gms. Split grams (*Chana dal*)
15 gms. Salt
12 gms. Red chillies powdered

6 gms. Cumin seeds
3 gms. Turmeric
25 gms. Garlic ground
3 gms. *Garam masala* powder

115 gms. Onions finely chopped
15 mls. (½ oz.) Vinegar
Ghee for frying the kababs.

• Wash and cut each goolar into four pieces. Soak them in deep water for two hours, stirring occasionally. By this process small insects, if present, will come out and float on the surface of the water, and can easily be drained off.

• In a separate pan boil fresh water and add goolar pieces along with split grams, salt, red chillies, cumin seeds, turmeric and garlic. When goolar and split grams are cooked, dry the liquid completely. Add *garam masala* powder. Grind it to fine paste. Divide into 24 equal parts.

• Add vinegar into the chopped onions and divide into 24 equal parts.

• Flatten each part of the goolar paste, put in its centre one part of chopped onions and shape into a ball. Flatten, wetting hands with a little water to give kababs a smooth and even shape. In a very little ghee fry on low heat till dark brown.

Shalgam ke Kabab

Preparation time: 30 minutes • Cooking time: 1½ hours • To serve: 8 persons.

2 kgs. Turnips (*Shalgam*) peeled

9 gms. Salt

6 gms. Red chillies powdered

1½ gms. *Garam masala* powder

60 gms. Parched grams powdered

115 gms. Onions thinly and evenly sliced

Ghee for frying kababs.

• Fry the sliced onions to a golden brown and grind dry. Cut each turnip (*Shalgam*) into four pieces. Boil them in water. When cooked, discard the water, take a few pieces, at a time, and wrap them in muslin. Squeeze tightly to extract as much liquid as possible. Discard the liquid. Grind the turnips finely. Add salt, red chillies, *garam masala*, parched grams and fried onions to the turnips, mix and knead well.

• Divide into 16 equal parts. Flatten, wetting hands with a little water to give kababs a smooth and even shape.

• In a very little ghee fry on low heat till golden brown.

• Kababs taste better if, when fried, they are kept for a few hours and slightly fried again before serving.

Lahasun ki Kheer

Another really unusual dish. A sweet made out of garlic. With the modern world now discovering the benefits of garlic, this should be welcome. Those not admiring garlic flavour can also be served this and not know.
I am grateful to Maharaj Ramchandra Singhji of Kushalgarh for giving me this fine recipe.

Preparation time: 1 hour ● Cooking time: 2 hours ● To serve: 6 – 8 persons.

120 gms. Garlic cloves, large peeled
12 gms. Alum (*Phitkari*) powdered

2 litres Milk
250 gms. Sugar
1½ gms. Cardamom seeds powdered

15 mls. (½ oz.) Rose water.

● Cut and discard both ends of the garlic cloves. Then cut each garlic in four pieces, lengthwise.
● Soak these pieces in deep water for one hour. Throw the water and again soak in fresh water for another hour.
● In a pan boil about 4 cups of water. Add half of the powdered alum, and stir. Add sliced garlic and boil for 10 minutes. Discard the water. Again take 4 cups of water, mix the remaining alum and boil sliced garlic for 10 minutes. Wash boiled garlic in fresh water. Keep aside.
● Boil milk till it reduces to half. Add garlic and sugar, and boil till it is of thick consistency. Add cardamom and rose water. Serve cold.

Dahi ka Halwa*

Preparation time: 1 hour • Cooking time: 1 hour • To serve: 8 – 10 persons.

1 kg. Curd, fresh and thick	1½ gms. Cardamom seeds powdered	60 mls. (2 ozs.) Rose water
120 gms. Ghee	1½ gms. Mace powdered	36 gms. Almonds blanched and shredded
120 gms. Semolina (*Sujji*)	A pinch of Saffron diluted in warm water	36 gms. Pistachios blanched and shredded.
250 gms. Sugar		

• Put the curd in muslin and hang it on a peg for 4 or 5 hours. On being drained, the curd should be 500 gms. in weight.

• Heat the ghee in a *kadhai*. Add semolina. Keep on stirring on low fire till it is of golden colour. Remove from fire, add curd and stir well. Then add sugar. Put back on fire and cook, stirring till it thickens and begins to come off the sides of the *kadhai*. Add cardamom, mace, saffron and rose water and stir well. Keep on fire for another 5 minutes.

• While serving dress with almonds and pistachios.

* Picture on page 176.

155

Gulab ki Kheer

Preparation time: 15 minutes • Cooking time: 1 hour • To serve: 6 – 8 persons.

50 gms. Fresh rose petals   2 litres Milk   250 gms. Sugar.

- Select Edward, Bussarah or any scented variety of roses. Pluck the petals discarding stigma, the central portion.
- Boil milk along with rose petals (whole), till it reduces to half. Add sugar and boil further till it is of thick consistency.
- Serve cold.

156

Makki ka Halwa

Preparation time: 15 minutes • Cooking time: 1 hour • To serve: 6 – 8 persons.

½ kg. Fresh corn kernels grated finely
250 gms. Ghee

½ litre Milk
60 gms. Coconut grated
½ kg. Sugar
60 gms. Raisins whole

3 gms. Cardamoms powdered.

- Take fresh and tender corns. Grate the kernels finely.
- Heat the ghee in a *kadhai*. Add grated kernels and cook on low fire stirring regularly to a deep golden colour. Add milk. When milk dries up, add grated coconut and mix well. Add sugar. When it thickens and begins to come off the sides of the *kadhai,* remove from fire. Add raisins and cardamoms and mix well.

Gosht ka Halwa

Halwa, the most common Indian sweet. To this my father gave this unusual turn. If Halwa can be made from dal, gajar, almonds etc. why not out of meat? After many experiments, this dish was born.

Preparation time: 1 hour ● Cooking time: 2 hours ● To serve: 6 – 8 persons.

½ kg. Minced lean mutton from leg *or* shoulder (*Keema*)
6 gms. Salt
250 gms. *Khoa*
250 gms. Ghee

3 gms. Cardamom seeds powdered
60 mls. (2 ozs.) Rose water *or* kewada water
A good pinch of Saffron, diluted in warm water

½ kg. Sugar powdered finely
50 gms. Almonds blanched and shredded
50 gms. Charoli blanched whole.

● Wash minced meat in water four times changing water every time. Drain
● Boil meat, with salt, in water. When tender, dry the water completely. Grind the meat very finely.
● Mix *khoa* into the meat.
● Heat the ghee and fry the meat on low fire till well-browned. Add cardamoms, rose water, saffron and sugar. Stir and at once remove from the fire. Then keep on stirring till the halwa absorbs the ghee.
● While serving decorate with almonds and charoli.

Ande ka Halwa

Excellent as a tonic on winter mornings.

Preparation time: 1 hour • Cooking time: 1 hour • To serve: 6 – 8 persons.

5 Large eggs hard boiled	1½ gms. Cardamom seeds powdered	12 gms. Pistachios blanched and shredded
60 gms. Ghee	A good pinch of Saffron diluted in warm water	12 gms. Charoli blanched whole
30 gms. Refined flour		
120 mls. (4 ozs.) Milk	15 mls. (½ oz.) Rose water	12 gms. Raisins cut into halves.
30 gms. *Khoa*	12 gms. Almonds blanched and shredded	
120 gms. Sugar		

• Chop the eggs and grind them very finely, without water. Heat the ghee in a *kadhai*. Add refined flour. Keep on stirring till golden brown. Add milk and mix well. Add ground eggs and *khoa* and mix well. Cook on low fire stirring regularly till the milk dries up. Add sugar. When it thickens and begins to come off the sides of the *kadhai*, add all the remaining ingredients, mix well and remove from fire.

• Can be preserved for a week. Reheat while serving.

Makki ki Firni

Preparation time: 30 minutes • Cooking time: 30 minutes • To serve: 6 – 8 persons.

½ kg. Fresh corn kernels grated
½ litre Milk

250 gms. Sugar
1½ gms. Cardamom seeds powdered

115 gms. Cream.

- Grate fresh and tender corn kernels and grind very finely.
- Add milk, sugar and cardamoms to the ground kernels, and stir well. Strain through a muslin and discard the residue.
- Cook on low fire stirring constantly to avoid lump formation. When thick remove from fire and cool it completely. Add cream and stir well.
- Serve cold.

Murakkat*

Preparation time: 30 minutes • Cooking time: 1½ hours • To serve: 6 – 8 persons.

2 litres Milk
60 gms. Basmati rice
250 gms. Sugar

25 gms. Almonds blanched and ground with water

60 gms. *Khoa.*

- Boil milk along with rice. When it starts thickening add sugar, almonds and *khoa*. Cook, stirring constantly, till it is of *halwa* consistency.
- Spread it evenly, to one inch thickness, on a baking pan.
- Put tawa or a flat metal plate on fire and over it put the baking pan. Cook on medium fire till it turns light brown. Cool and cut into squares.
- Serve cold.

* Picture on page 176.

Dahi ka Bhajia*

Preparation time: 30 minutes • Cooking time: 1 hour • To serve: 6 – 8 persons.

1 kg. Curd, fresh and thick
120 gms. Refined flour
3 gms. Cuttle bones *Samandar-jhag)* finely powdered

500 gms. Sugar
1½ gms. Cardamom seeds powdered
A pinch of Saffron diluted in warm water

Ghee for deep frying *bhajias.*

• Put curd in muslin and hang it on a peg for 4 or 5 hours. On being drained the curd should be 500 gms. in weight.
• Add refined flour and powdered cuttle bones to the curd and mix thoroughly. If the mixture is too thick for making *bhajias,* add whey, the dripped water of the curd, as much as necessary.
• In a separate pan put sugar and four cups of water. Cook, stirring till the syrup gets 2-threads consistency. Add powdered cardamoms and saffron. Keep warm on hot ashes.
• Heat the ghee in *kadhai* and deep fry *bhajias,* of medium size, on medium fire till dark brown.
• Put them in sugar syrup. When they sink to the bottom of the pan, remove and serve.

162

Nimish

This Recipe is very popular with children and tastes even better if served in clay cups (Sakroas).

To serve 6 – 8 persons.

1½ litre Buffalo milk
175 gms. Sugar

1½ gms. Cuttle bones *(Samandar-jhag)* finely powdered

15 mls. (½ oz.) Rose water.

• Boil the milk, then cool it. Mix sugar, cuttle bones and rose water. Stir well. Cover and keep in refrigerator to cool (not freeze).
• After 12 hours remove from refrigerator and beat the milk with an egg-beater to form foam. As the foam rises remove it with a spoon, being careful not to take any milk. Serve the foam right away. Continue beating till foam stops forming.

* Picture on page 176.

Gajar Halwa Ala Kism

Preparation time: 30 minutes • Cooking time: 1 hour • To serve: 6 – 8 persons.

500 gms. Carrots scraped and core removed	500 gms. Sugar	60 gms. Almonds blanched and shredded
1 litre Milk	120 gms. Rice powdered	60 gms. Raisins cut into
120 gms. *Malai*	120 gms. Ghee	two pieces.

• Scrape the carrots, cut and remove both ends. Then cut into halves lengthwise, and remove the hard core from the middle. Cut into 1" pieces.
• Boil carrots in milk. When tender, dry the milk completely. Grind carrots finely.
• In a *kadhai* heat the ghee, add carrots, *malai*, sugar and rice powder, and cook on low fire, stirring regularly till of thick consistency. Serve at once. While serving, dress with almonds and raisins.

164

Hare Chane ka Halwa

Preparation time: 30 minutes • Cooking time: 1 hour • To serve: 6 – 8 persons.

½ kg. Fresh green grams   60 gms. Wheat flour   150 gms. Sugar.
175 gms. Ghee   ½ litre Milk

● Boil green grams in about 2 cups of water. When tender, dry up the water. Grind the grams very finely.
● In a *kadhai*, heat the ghee. Add wheat flour and fry it to golden colour. Add grams and cook on low fire, stirring regularly. When they stop sticking at the bottom of the *kadhai*, add milk and stir. When milk dries up, add sugar. When thick and begins to come off the sides of the *kadhai*, remove from fire.